Dear Friends,

Dinner does not get much easier than a meal cooked all in one pot. And, in this book filled with a variety of delicious recipes, you're sure to find foods, flavors and cooking methods that suit your mood and meal occasion. Plus, because all of the meal is in one dish, nothing more is needed to complete dinner—if you choose to add a salad or bread, it's just an added bonus!

So for a hearty dinner cooked all in one pot, look no further. There are easy skillet meals and soups that can be made at the last minute, and satisfying casseroles, roasted meals and pot pies to pop into the oven for later. Plus, go ahead and savor fabulously tasty slow cooker dinners that allow your time to be freed up until just before dinner.

The Big Book of One-Pot Dinners is filled with more than 200 easy, delicious recipes chosen to please, all with the easy preparation and minimal cleanup that cooking in one dish offers. You'll love the familiar but trendy flavors and the fabulous variety throughout the recipes. Plus, as a special feature, each chapter includes a favorite "heirloom" recipe with a companion "new twist" recipe for you to try. The "new twist" is similar to the original but offers something new and different—be sure to try them all!

This cookbook answers the question "What's for dinner?" with an amazing array of recipe choices, each one creatively made in just one pot.

Perfect for groups of 8 or more — **crowd-pleasing**

Main dishes with 400 calories or less — **calorie-controlled**

Eat Hearty!
Betty Crocker

contents

Just One Pot • 6

just one pot

One-Pot Cookware for All Cooks

Consider the varieties of one-pot cookware that are available, and you might be overwhelmed by the magnitude of what you can use. If you are an experienced cook, you might already have favorites, but it's always fun to dream about that new beautiful casserole or a better-quality skillet. Plus, for one-pot dinners, you might want to serve the meal right from the pot, so appearance might make a difference.

When you are choosing new cookware for your one-pot dinners, expect prices to vary widely, all based on materials, use and sometimes even brand. In general, higher-quality materials will demand a higher price, but often you can purchase cookware that is quite nice in the medium price range. Also consider weight — lighter, easier-to-handle cookware may be easier for you to use, and heaviness does not necessarily mean better. You'll want to choose pieces that are easy to keep clean, cook evenly and are the correct size for your family and the recipes that you are using.

Skillet and Saucepan Choices

It's nice to have a variety of skillets and saucepans for different uses. You can choose to purchase sets of pans or individual pieces in different materials.

- Stainless Steel
- Nonstick
- Cast Iron

Dutch Oven Choices

These heavy pots with thick walls are ideal for cooking soups and stews and can be used on the stovetop and in the oven. If you don't have a Dutch oven, a stainless steel stockpot or other large pot can be substituted with most foods. These elegant cooking pots come fitted with a tight cover.

- Cast Iron
- Enameled Cast Iron

Casserole Choices

Mainly for use in the oven, this bakeware comes in a variety of sizes and materials. If you are not sure of the size of your casserole dish, simply fill with water, then measure the water to get a cup amount. Many casserole dishes come with a cover, but foil can be used if you don't have one for the dish you are using. Soufflé dishes with high sides as well as gratin dishes can be used for casseroles too and are attractive for serving at the table.

- Stoneware
- Glass
- Ceramic

Pie Plate and Pan Choices

These typically round dishes come in a variety of sizes, but 9-inch and 10-inch are the most common. Deep-dish pie plates are available too and are nice to have on hand for recipes that require a little more depth. Just for fun, look for colorful pie plates or those with scalloped or other decorative edges.

- Stoneware
- Glass
- Ceramic
- Aluminum

Slow Cooker How-To

Wouldn't it be great to walk in the front door after a long day to find a warm, hearty meal ready and waiting? That homemade dinner dream can be a reality when you rely on the convenience of your slow cooker. Just check out our tips and the great recipes starting on page 228, and you'll be on the way to delicious, easy meals.

Slow Cooker Features

Manufacturers offer slow cookers in a variety of shapes and sizes, and with an array of features. Most models range in size from 3½ to 8 quarts. For the best results, use the size recommended in the recipe you are using. Here are some of the most common features:

- **Continuous** — The majority of slow cookers are continuous, meaning they cook foods continuously using very low wattage. The heating coils are on constantly to heat the ceramic insert. These models have two to four fixed settings (Low, High, Warm and sometimes Auto).

- **Programmable** — These models offer one-touch control with multiple time and temperature settings.

- **Multi-compartment** — These slow cookers have either two or three cooking compartments with individual heat settings.

- **Portable** — These models have locking lids, carrying handles and even travel bags to transport the slow cooker.

- **Intermittent** — These cookers have a heating element in the base and a separate cooking container on the base. The heat cycles on and off to maintain a constant temperature.

Tips for Slow Cooker Success

Follow these easy tips and you'll be a slow cooking expert in no time!

- For easy cleanup, coat the inside of the slow cooker insert with cooking spray.

- Slow cookers are the most efficient when they are two-thirds to three-fourths full.

- Always keep the slow cooker covered for the time stated in the recipe. Removing the cover allows heat to escape, adding 15 to 20 minutes to the cook time. Only remove the cover if a recipe specifies and only after the first 2 hours of cooking.

- Cut most ingredients into uniform sizes for the best cooking results.

- Root vegetables take longer to cook than other vegetables, so cut them into smaller pieces and place at the bottom of the slow cooker.

- Make sure raw potatoes are covered with liquid to prevent them from darkening.

- Don't add more liquid than specified. Liquids don't evaporate from a slow cooker and food will remain moist.

- Remove poultry skin and excess fat from meats before cooking to reduce fat in the dish.

- Brown meat and poultry in a skillet before adding to the slow cooker to add flavor and color.

Jazzing Up Slow Cooked Dinners

Long slow cooking times often cause colors to dull and flavors to merge. To add some spark to your finished meal, try one of these easy toppers.

- Chopped fresh herbs, whole herb leaves or herb sprigs
- Chopped or sliced avocado, onion, bell pepper, chiles or tomato
- Citrus zest or strips
- Cubed, diced, shaved, shredded, grated or crumbled cheese
- Coarsely broken or crushed potato, tortilla or corn chips
- Whole or coarsely crushed croutons
- Small-size savory snack mixes
- Crumbled, crisply cooked bacon
- Toasted or untoasted nuts
- Sour cream or plain yogurt

CHAPTER
1

casseroles

chicken-artichoke casserole

prep time: 15 Minutes || **start to finish:** 50 Minutes || 6 servings (1⅓ cups each)

1 tablespoon olive oil

1 medium red bell pepper, chopped (1 cup)

4 medium green onions, sliced (¼ cup)

3 cups chopped cooked chicken

1 can (14 oz) artichoke hearts, drained, chopped

1 container (10 oz) refrigerated reduced-fat Alfredo pasta sauce

1 cup shredded Asiago cheese (4 oz)

½ cup reduced-fat mayonnaise

1½ cups Romano cheese croutons (from 5-oz bag), coarsely crushed

Additional sliced green onions, if desired

1 Heat oven to 350°F. Spray 11x7-inch (2-quart) glass baking dish with cooking spray.

2 In 6- to 8-inch skillet, heat oil over medium heat. Add bell pepper and green onions; cook 2 to 3 minutes, stirring occasionally, until vegetables begin to soften. In large bowl, mix bell pepper mixture and all remaining ingredients except croutons and additional green onions. Spoon into baking dish. Top with croutons.

3 Bake uncovered 30 to 35 minutes or until hot and bubbly. Sprinkle with additional sliced green onions before serving.

1 Serving: Calories 460; Total Fat 28g (Saturated Fat 11g, Trans Fat 1g); Cholesterol 105mg; Sodium 890mg; Total Carbohydrate 20g (Dietary Fiber 4g); Protein 30g **Exchanges:** 1 Starch, 1 Vegetable, 3½ Medium-Fat Meat, 2 Fat **Carbohydrate Choices:** 1

Quick Variation If refrigerated Alfredo sauce is not available, use about 1 cup of Alfredo sauce from a jar.

cheesy chicken enchilada casserole

prep time: 20 Minutes ‖ **start to finish:** 55 Minutes ‖ 8 servings

2 cups diced cooked chicken

1 can (15.5 oz) pinto beans, drained, rinsed

½ cup chunky-style salsa

3 teaspoons chili powder

¼ teaspoon garlic powder

½ loaf (16-oz size) prepared cheese product, cut into cubes

1 cup Original Bisquick™ mix

¾ cup milk

2 tablespoons butter, melted

1 cup shredded lettuce

1 plum (Roma) tomato, diced (½ cup)

4 medium green onions, sliced (¼ cup)

Guacamole, if desired

Sour cream, if desired

Sliced pickled jalapeño chiles, if desired

1 Heat oven to 425°F. Spray round 2-quart casserole or 11x7-inch glass baking dish with cooking spray.

2 In large bowl, mix chicken, beans, salsa, chili powder and garlic powder; stir in cheese. Spoon into casserole. In small bowl, mix Bisquick mix, milk and butter. Pour and spoon evenly over chicken mixture.

3 Bake 30 to 35 minutes or until crust is golden brown. Top with lettuce, tomato and green onions. Serve with guacamole, sour cream and sliced pickled jalapeño chiles.

1 Serving: Calories 350; Total Fat 16g (Saturated Fat 9g, Trans Fat 1g); Cholesterol 65mg; Sodium 610mg; Total Carbohydrate 28g (Dietary Fiber 6g); Protein 24g **Exchanges:** 1½ Starch, ½ Vegetable, 2½ Medium-Fat Meat, ½ Fat **Carbohydrate Choices:** 2

Quick Variations Use leftover chicken or rotisserie chicken in this recipe, or look for diced cooked chicken in the refrigerator or freezer case of the grocery store.

Try 1 can (15 oz) black beans in place of the pinto beans.

chicken enchilada casserole

prep time: 20 Minutes ‖ start to finish: 55 Minutes ‖ 3 servings

1 boneless skinless chicken breast, cut into thin bite-size strips

½ medium red bell pepper, finely chopped

¼ teaspoon ground cumin

1 can (18.5 oz) ready-to-serve light Southwestern-style vegetable soup

¼ cup uncooked instant brown rice

1 oz fat-free cream cheese, cut into cubes

3 tablespoons fat-free refried beans (from 16-oz can)

4 corn tortillas (6-inch)

⅓ cup shredded reduced-fat mild Cheddar cheese

1 Heat oven to 350°F. In 12-inch nonstick skillet, cook chicken and bell pepper over medium-high heat 4 to 6 minutes, stirring constantly, until chicken begins to brown and bell pepper is crisp-tender. Sprinkle with cumin.

2 Stir in soup. Heat to boiling. Stir in rice; reduce heat to low. Cover; cook 10 minutes or until rice is tender.

3 Stir cream cheese into chicken mixture until well blended. Spread 1 tablespoon of the refried beans on 1 tortilla; place, beans side up, in bottom of ungreased 1-quart casserole. Top with 1 cup of the chicken mixture; sprinkle with 1 tablespoon of the cheese. Repeat 2 times. Top with remaining tortilla; sprinkle with remaining cheese.

4 Cover; bake 20 to 25 minutes or until mixture is hot and cheese is melted.

1 Serving: Calories 250; Total Fat 35g (Saturated Fat 1g, Trans Fat 0g); Cholesterol 30mg; Sodium 880mg; Total Carbohydrate 35g (Dietary Fiber 6g); Protein 19g **Exchanges:** 2 Starch, ½ Other Carbohydrate, 2 Very Lean Meat **Carbohydrate Choices:** 2

make it ahead Make the casserole up to 24 hours ahead of baking and store covered in the refrigerator. Since you'll be baking a cold casserole, expect the bake time to be a few minutes longer.

creamy pesto-chicken casserole

prep time: 20 Minutes ‖ **start to finish:** 55 Minutes ‖ 4 servings (1½ cups each)

2 cups uncooked radiatore (nuggets) pasta (6 oz)

½ cup chopped drained roasted red bell peppers (from 7-oz jar)

⅓ cup basil pesto

¼ cup fat-free (skim) milk

1 container (10 oz) refrigerated reduced-fat Alfredo pasta sauce

2 packages (6 oz each) refrigerated grilled chicken breast strips, chopped

¼ cup shredded Parmesan cheese (1 oz)

1 Heat oven to 350°F. Spray 8-inch square (2-quart) glass baking dish with cooking spray.

2 Cook pasta 9 minutes as directed on package. Drain; return to saucepan. Stir in all remaining ingredients except cheese. Spoon into baking dish.

3 Cover with foil. Bake 35 minutes. Sprinkle with cheese before serving.

1 Serving: Calories 560; Total Fat 25g (Saturated Fat 9g, Trans Fat 0g); Cholesterol 90mg; Sodium 1210mg; Total Carbohydrate 46g (Dietary Fiber 2g); Protein 37g **Exchanges:** 3 Starch, 4 Lean Meat, 2½ Fat **Carbohydrate Choices:** 3

Quick Variation Although using the refrigerated chicken strips is convenient, you can also use 2½ cups of any cooked chicken.

make it ahead Go ahead and cook the pasta the night (or morning) before dinner as directed in step 2. Drain and rinse with cold water. Drizzle with 1 teaspoon olive oil, and refrigerate in a large food-storage plastic bag or container. You can assemble the casserole in 5 minutes!

country chicken and pasta bake

prep time: **10 Minutes** || start to finish: **40 Minutes** || **6 servings**

2 cups uncooked radiatore (nuggets) pasta (6 oz)

3 cups cubed cooked chicken

2 jars (12 oz each) chicken gravy

1 bag (1 lb) frozen broccoli, carrots and cauliflower

¼ teaspoon dried thyme leaves

¼ teaspoon salt

½ cup herb-seasoned stuffing crumbs

2 tablespoons butter, melted

1 Heat oven to 375°F. Cook and drain pasta as directed on package, using minimum cook time.

2 In ungreased 2½-quart casserole, mix pasta and all remaining ingredients except stuffing and butter.

3 Cover; bake 20 minutes. Uncover; stir casserole. In small bowl, mix stuffing and butter; sprinkle over top. Bake uncovered about 10 minutes longer or until hot and topping is browned.

1 Serving: Calories 410; Total Fat 16g (Saturated Fat 6g, Trans Fat 0g); Cholesterol 75mg; Sodium 1030mg; Total Carbohydrate 38g (Dietary Fiber 4g); Protein 28g **Exchanges:** 2 Starch, 1 Vegetable, 3 Medium-Fat Meat **Carbohydrate Choices:** 2½

Quick Variation Any frozen vegetable mixture can be used, and with so many choices now available, we know you're likely to keep your favorites on hand.

easy herb-chicken bake

prep time: 20 Minutes || **start to finish:** 50 Minutes || 8 servings

FILLING

- 1 tablespoon butter
- ½ cup chopped onion (1 medium)
- ½ cup chopped celery
- ½ cup chopped red bell pepper
- ½ teaspoon seasoned salt
- 2 cups cubed cooked chicken or turkey
- 1 bag (12 oz) frozen extra-sweet whole kernel corn
- 1 can (10¾ oz) condensed cream of chicken soup

CRUST

- 1 cup Original Bisquick mix
- ¼ cup milk
- ¾ cup shredded Cheddar cheese (3 oz)
- ¾ teaspoon dried thyme leaves

1 Heat oven to 400°F. Spray 8-inch square (2-quart) glass baking dish with cooking spray.

2 In 10-inch skillet, melt butter over medium-high heat. Add onion, celery, bell pepper and seasoned salt; cook about 5 minutes, stirring occasionally, until vegetables are tender. Stir in chicken, corn and soup; cook and stir until hot.

3 In medium bowl, mix Bisquick mix, milk, ½ cup of the cheese and the thyme. With floured fingers, press crust mixture evenly over bottom and 1 inch up sides of baking dish. Spoon hot filling into crust.

4 Bake 22 to 30 minutes or until crust is golden brown. Sprinkle top with remaining ¼ cup cheese. To serve, cut into squares.

1 Serving: Calories 270; Total Fat 12g (Saturated Fat 5g, Trans Fat 1g); Cholesterol 50mg; Sodium 660mg; Total Carbohydrate 23g (Dietary Fiber 2g); Protein 16g **Exchanges:** 1½ Starch, 1½ Lean Meat, 1½ Fat **Carbohydrate Choices:** 1½

Quick Variation If you have leftover rotisserie chicken or turkey from the deli, this recipe is ideal for using it up.

country french chicken and rice

¼ cup chopped sun-dried tomatoes in oil, drained

2 tablespoons herbes de Provence

2 tablespoons olive oil

2 tablespoons lemon juice

1 tablespoon finely chopped garlic

1 teaspoon salt

8 bone-in chicken thighs (about 2 lb), skin and fat removed

1½ cups sliced fresh mushrooms (4 oz)

1 cup uncooked regular long-grain white rice

1 medium carrot, shredded (½ cup)

2 cups boiling water

1 tablespoon chopped fresh Italian (flat-leaf) parsley

2 teaspoons grated lemon peel

1 In 1-gallon resealable food-storage plastic bag, mix tomatoes, herbes de Provence, oil, lemon juice, garlic and ½ teaspoon of the salt. Add chicken thighs and mushrooms; seal bag. Turn to coat thighs and mushrooms in marinade. Refrigerate at least 2 hours but no longer than 24 hours.

2 Heat oven to 375°F. Spray 13x9-inch (3-quart) glass baking dish with cooking spray. In baking dish, place rice, carrot and remaining ½ teaspoon salt; stir in boiling water. Pour chicken thighs, mushrooms and marinade evenly over rice mixture.

3 Cover with foil. Bake 50 to 60 minutes or until liquid is absorbed and juice of chicken is clear when thickest part is cut to bone (at least 165°F). Sprinkle with parsley and lemon peel.

1 Serving: Calories 260; Total Fat 10g (Saturated Fat 25g, Trans Fat 0g); Cholesterol 45mg; Sodium 360mg; Total Carbohydrate 23g (Dietary Fiber 1g); Protein 18g **Exchanges:** 1½ Starch, 2 Lean Meat, ½ Fat **Carbohydrate Choices:** 1½

Quick Variation If herbes de Provence is not available, use any combination of dried basil, fennel seed, lavender, marjoram, rosemary, sage, summer savory, tarragon or thyme.

buffalo chicken and potatoes

prep time: **10 Minutes** || start to finish: **1 Hour 5 Minutes** || **6 servings (1¾ cups each)**

1¼ **lb boneless skinless chicken breasts, cut into 1-inch strips**

⅓ **cup buffalo wing sauce**

6 **cups frozen southern-style diced hash brown potatoes, thawed**

1 **cup ranch or blue cheese dressing**

½ **cup shredded Cheddar cheese (2 oz)**

1 **can (10 oz) condensed cream of celery soup**

½ **cup corn flake crumbs**

2 **tablespoons butter, melted**

¼ **cup chopped green onions (3 or 4 medium)**

1 Heat oven to 350°F. Spray 13x9-inch (3-quart) glass baking dish with cooking spray.

2 In medium bowl, stir together chicken strips and wing sauce.

3 In large bowl, stir together potatoes, dressing, cheese and soup. Spoon into baking dish. Place chicken strips in single layer over potato mixture.

4 In small bowl, stir together crumbs and butter. Sprinkle over top.

5 Cover with foil. Bake 30 minutes. Uncover; bake 20 to 25 minutes longer or until potatoes are tender and juice of chicken is no longer pink when centers of thickest pieces are cut. Sprinkle with green onions.

1 Serving: Calories 620; Total Fat 33g (Saturated Fat 9g, Trans Fat 0g); Cholesterol 90mg; Sodium 1240mg; Total Carbohydrate 51g (Dietary Fiber 5g); Protein 28g **Exchanges:** 2½ Starch, 1 Other Carbohydrate, 3 Lean Meat, 4½ Fat **Carbohydrate Choices:** 3½

Quick Variations For authentic flavor, go with red hot buffalo wing sauce. Other flavors to try include teriyaki, sweet and sour or barbecue.

For a cheesy hash brown side dish, omit the chicken and wing sauce. Serve the casserole with barbecued chicken or baked ham.

time-saver Try using precut chicken tenders to make prep time shorter.

chicken-vegetable tetrazzini

prep time: 20 Minutes || **start to finish:** 50 Minutes || **6 servings**

7 oz uncooked whole wheat or multigrain spaghetti, broken into thirds

½ cup frozen shelled edamame (from 10-oz bag)

1 cup 1-inch diagonal pieces fresh asparagus

2 tablespoons butter

1 cup sliced fresh mushrooms (3 oz)

¼ cup all-purpose flour

½ teaspoon salt

¼ teaspoon pepper

1 cup chicken broth (from 32-oz carton)

1 cup fat-free half-and-half

2 tablespoons dry sherry or water

2 cups cubed or shredded deli rotisserie chicken (from 2- to 3-lb chicken)

½ cup chopped orange, yellow or red bell pepper

¼ cup shredded Parmesan or Asiago cheese (1 oz)

1 Heat oven to 350°F. Cook spaghetti as directed on package, adding edamame and asparagus during last 3 minutes of cooking time; drain.

2 Meanwhile, in 2-quart saucepan, melt butter over medium heat. Add mushrooms; cook just until tender. Remove from saucepan with slotted spoon; set aside. Stir flour, salt and pepper into same saucepan. Gradually stir in broth until mixture is smooth. Stir in half-and-half. Heat to boiling, stirring constantly. Boil and stir 1 minute.

3 Add mushrooms, spaghetti and vegetables, sherry, chicken and bell pepper to sauce; stir until combined. Spoon into ungreased 2-quart casserole.

4 Bake uncovered 20 minutes. Sprinkle with cheese; bake about 10 minutes longer or until bubbly in center.

1 Serving: Calories 340; Total Fat 11g (Saturated Fat 5g, Trans Fat 0g); Cholesterol 60mg; Sodium 780mg; Total Carbohydrate 37g (Dietary Fiber 4g); Protein 22g **Exchanges:** 2½ Starch, ½ Vegetable, 2 Lean Meat, ½ Fat **Carbohydrate Choices:** 2½

Quick Variation Substitute cubed cooked turkey for the chicken and frozen sweet peas for the edamame.

fiesta taco casserole

prep time: 15 Minutes ‖ **start to finish:** 45 Minutes ‖ **4 servings**

1 lb lean (at least 80%) ground beef

1 can (15 to 16 oz) spicy chili beans in sauce, undrained

1 cup chunky-style salsa

2 cups coarsely broken tortilla chips

4 medium green onions, sliced (¼ cup)

1 medium tomato, chopped (¾ cup)

1 cup shredded Cheddar or Monterey Jack cheese (4 oz)

Tortilla chips, if desired

Shredded lettuce, if desired

Additional chunky-style salsa, if desired

1 Heat oven to 350°F. In 10-inch skillet, cook beef over medium heat 8 to 10 minutes, stirring occasionally, until browned; drain. Stir in beans and 1 cup salsa. Heat to boiling, stirring occasionally.

2 In ungreased 2-quart casserole, place broken tortilla chips. Top with beef mixture. Sprinkle with green onions, tomato and cheese.

3 Bake uncovered 20 to 30 minutes or until hot and bubbly. Arrange tortilla chips around edge of casserole. Serve with lettuce and additional salsa.

1 Serving: Calories 530; Total Fat 27g (Saturated Fat 11g, Trans Fat 1g); Cholesterol 100mg; Sodium 1540mg; Total Carbohydrate 36g (Dietary Fiber 7g); Protein 35g **Exchanges:** 2 Starch, ½ Other Carbohydrate, 4 Medium-Fat Meat, 1 Fat **Carbohydrate Choices:** 2½

healthy twist To reduce the fat to about 19 grams and the calories to about 470 per serving, use ground turkey breast and reduced-fat Cheddar cheese.

potato-topped meat loaf casserole

prep time: **20 Minutes** ‖ start to finish: **55 Minutes** ‖ **6 servings**

MEAT LOAF

- 1 **lb extra-lean (at least 90%) ground beef**
- 3 **tablespoons unseasoned dry bread crumbs**
- 1 **egg**
- 3 **tablespoons steak sauce**
- 1 **tablespoon dried minced onion**
- ½ **teaspoon salt**
- ¼ **teaspoon pepper**

FILLING

- 1¾ **cups water**
- ½ **cup milk**
- 2 **tablespoons butter**
- ¼ **teaspoon salt**
- 2 **cups dry plain mashed potato mix**
- 1 **egg**
- 1½ **cups frozen chopped broccoli, thawed**
- ½ **cup shredded sharp Cheddar cheese (2 oz)**

1 Heat oven to 350°F. Spray 8-inch square (2-quart) glass baking dish with cooking spray. In medium bowl, mix meat loaf ingredients. Press in bottom and up sides of baking dish to within ½ inch of top.

2 In 2-quart saucepan, heat water, milk, butter and salt to boiling. Remove from heat; stir in potato mix. Let stand 30 seconds. Stir in egg. Stir in broccoli and cheese. Spoon into meat shell, spreading evenly.

3 Bake 25 to 30 minutes or until meat loaf is thoroughly cooked and meat thermometer inserted in center of meat reads 160°F. Let stand 5 minutes before serving; drain drippings from baking dish.

1 Serving: Calories 330; Total Fat 15g (Saturated Fat 8g, Trans Fat 0.5g); Cholesterol 140mg; Sodium 610mg; Total Carbohydrate 26g (Dietary Fiber 2g); Protein 23g **Exchanges:** 1½ Starch, 2½ Medium-Fat Meat, ½ Fat **Carbohydrate Choices:** 2

time-saver Purchase refrigerated mashed potatoes for this recipe. Add the egg, broccoli and cheese as directed.

philly cheese and ground beef casserole

prep time: 20 Minutes ‖ **start to finish:** 1 Hour ‖ 8 servings

1½ lb lean (at least 80%) ground beef

1 package (8 oz) sliced fresh mushrooms (about 3 cups)

1 teaspoon salt

½ teaspoon pepper

8 slices (1 oz each) provolone cheese

2 tablespoons butter

2 large onions, halved, thinly sliced into wedges

2 medium red bell peppers, cut into strips

2 cloves garlic, finely chopped

1 can (16.3 oz) refrigerated home-style original biscuits

1 Heat oven to 350°F. Spray 13x9-inch (3-quart) glass baking dish with cooking spray.

2 In 12-inch skillet, cook beef, mushrooms, salt and pepper over medium-high heat 7 to 9 minutes, stirring frequently, until beef is thoroughly cooked; drain. Place in baking dish. Arrange cheese over beef mixture, overlapping slices if needed.

3 In same skillet, melt butter over medium-high heat. Add onions and bell peppers; cook 3 to 5 minutes, stirring frequently, until peppers are crisp-tender. Stir in garlic; cook 1 to 2 minutes longer. Spoon over cheese in baking dish.

4 Separate dough into 8 biscuits. On lightly floured surface, pat biscuits into 5-inch rounds. Arrange biscuits over vegetable mixture.

5 Bake 35 to 40 minutes or until biscuits are golden brown on top.

1 Serving: Calories 490; Total Fat 28g (Saturated Fat 13g, Trans Fat 4g); Cholesterol 80mg; Sodium 1200mg; Total Carbohydrate 31g (Dietary Fiber 1g); Protein 27g **Exchanges:** 1½ Starch, 1½ Vegetable, 2½ Medium-Fat Meat, 3 Fat **Carbohydrate Choices:** 2

cheesy lasagna-stuffed peppers

prep time: 15 Minutes ‖ **start to finish:** 35 Minutes ‖ 4 servings

4 red or orange bell peppers

½ lb lean (at least 80%) ground beef

1⅔ cups milk

1 cup hot water

1 box Hamburger Helper™ four-cheese lasagna

¼ cup shredded Colby–Monterey Jack cheese blend or mozzarella cheese (1 oz)

Crushed red pepper flakes, if desired

1 Heat oven to 375°F. Cut tops off peppers; discard tops. Remove seeds and membranes; discard. Place bell peppers on ungreased cookie sheet.

2 In 10-inch nonstick skillet, cook beef over medium-high heat, stirring frequently, until browned; drain. Stir in milk, hot water, sauce mix and uncooked pasta (from Hamburger Helper box). Heat to boiling, stirring occasionally.

3 Reduce heat. Cover; simmer 6 to 8 minutes, stirring occasionally, until pasta is tender. Remove from heat. Spoon mixture into peppers. Top each with 1 tablespoon cheese.

4 Bake 15 to 20 minutes or until peppers are tender and cheese is melted. Sprinkle with red pepper flakes before serving.

1 Serving: Calories 360; Total Fat 12g (Saturated Fat 5g, Trans Fat 0.5g); Cholesterol 50mg; Sodium 1200mg; Total Carbohydrate 45g (Dietary Fiber 2g); Protein 20g **Exchanges:** 1 Starch, 1 Other Carbohydrate, ½ Low-Fat Milk, 1½ Vegetable, 1½ Lean Meat, 1 Fat **Carbohydrate Choices:** 3

spinach and beef enchiladas

prep time: 25 Minutes ‖ **start to finish:** 1 Hour 10 Minutes ‖ 8 servings (1 enchilada each)

1 lb lean (at least 80%) ground beef

1 medium onion, chopped (½ cup)

1 box (9 oz) frozen spinach

1 can (4.5 oz) chopped green chiles, undrained

½ teaspoon ground cumin

½ teaspoon garlic-pepper blend

½ cup sour cream

2 cups shredded Colby–Monterey Jack cheese blend (8 oz)

1 can (10 oz) enchilada sauce

1 package (11.5 oz) flour tortillas (8 tortillas)

½ cup chunky-style salsa

1 Heat oven to 350°F. Spray 13x9-inch (3-quart) glass baking dish with cooking spray. In 12-inch nonstick skillet, cook beef and onion over medium-high heat 5 to 7 minutes, stirring occasionally, until beef is browned.

2 Stir in spinach; cook, stirring frequently, until thawed. Stir in green chiles, cumin, garlic-pepper blend, sour cream and 1 cup of the cheese.

3 Spread about 1 teaspoon enchilada sauce on each tortilla. Top each with about ½ cup beef mixture. Roll up tortillas; place seam side down in baking dish. In small bowl, mix remaining enchilada sauce and the salsa; spoon over enchiladas. Sprinkle with remaining 1 cup cheese.

4 Spray sheet of foil with cooking spray; cover baking dish with foil. Bake 40 to 45 minutes or until thoroughly heated.

1 Serving: Calories 400; Total Fat 23g (Saturated Fat 11g, Trans Fat 0.5g); Cholesterol 70mg; Sodium 860mg; Total Carbohydrate 28g (Dietary Fiber 0g); Protein 21g **Exchanges:** 2 Starch, 2 High-Fat Meat, 1 Fat **Carbohydrate Choices:** 2

time-saver Who can resist a hot, bubbly pan of enchiladas? And these are so easy to make! Buying ground beef in bulk can save you money—just remember to divide it into smaller portions before freezing so you can defrost just the amount you need.

barbecue beef and bow-tie dinner

prep time: 15 Minutes | **start to finish:** 30 Minutes | **4 servings**

1 lb lean (at least 80%) ground beef

1 medium red bell pepper, chopped (1 cup)

1½ cups uncooked mini bow-tie (tripolini) pasta (5 oz)

2½ cups beef broth (from 32-oz carton)

½ cup barbecue sauce

½ teaspoon salt

¼ teaspoon pepper

1 cup frozen whole kernel corn, thawed

1½ cups shredded Cheddar cheese (6 oz)

1 In 12-inch nonstick skillet, cook beef over medium-high heat 5 to 7 minutes, stirring occasionally, until thoroughly cooked; drain.

2 Add bell pepper; cook and stir 1 minute. Stir in pasta, broth, barbecue sauce, salt and pepper. Heat to boiling. Reduce heat to medium-low; cover and cook 15 minutes, stirring occasionally, until pasta is tender.

3 Stir in corn and 1 cup of the cheese. Top with remaining ½ cup cheese. Cover; cook 3 to 4 minutes longer or until corn is hot and cheese is melted.

1 Serving: Calories 680; Total Fat 28g (Saturated Fat 14g, Trans Fat 1g); Cholesterol 115mg; Sodium 1470mg; Total Carbohydrate 66g (Dietary Fiber 4g); Protein 40g **Exchanges:** 4 Starch, ½ Vegetable, 3 High-Fat Meat, 1 Fat **Carbohydrate Choices:** 4½

time-saver Buy a block of Cheddar cheese when it's on sale; shred and store, tightly sealed, in the freezer. It will be handy whenever you need it for a recipe.

italian three-bean and sausage casserole

prep time: **20 Minutes** ‖ start to finish: **1 Hour 5 Minutes** ‖ **6 servings (1⅓ cups each)**

1 lb bulk spicy Italian pork sausage

1 large red bell pepper, chopped (1½ cups)

1 medium onion, chopped (½ cup)

1 large clove garlic, finely chopped

2 cans (15 oz each) cannellini beans, drained, rinsed

1 can (15.5 oz) great northern beans, drained, rinsed

1 can (15 to 16 oz) garbanzo beans, drained, rinsed

1 jar (1 lb 10 oz) tomato pasta sauce with basil and garlic

1½ teaspoons chopped fresh or ½ teaspoon dried basil leaves

Additional chopped fresh basil

1 Heat oven to 400°F. In 10-inch skillet, cook sausage, bell pepper, onion and garlic over medium heat 8 to 10 minutes, stirring occasionally, until sausage is no longer pink; drain.

2 In ungreased 3-quart casserole, mix sausage mixture and all remaining ingredients except additional basil.

3 Bake uncovered about 45 minutes, stirring once, until hot and bubbly. Garnish with additional basil.

1 Serving: Calories 530; Total Fat 14g (Saturated Fat 35g, Trans Fat 0g); Cholesterol 30mg; Sodium 1230mg; Total Carbohydrate 70g (Dietary Fiber 17g); Protein 30g **Exchanges:** 3 Starch, 1½ Other Carbohydrate, 1½ Very Lean Meat, 1½ High-Fat Meat **Carbohydrate Choices:** 4½

andouille sausage, squash and wild rice casserole

prep time: **25 Minutes** || start to finish: **2 Hours 30 Minutes** || **4 servings (1½ cups each)**

CASSEROLE

- 1 cup uncooked wild rice
- 2½ cups water
- 2 cups cubed (½-inch) butternut squash (about 10 oz)
- 1 link smoked andouille sausage (from 13.5-oz package), cut in half lengthwise, then crosswise into ¼-inch slices
- 1 can (10¾ oz) condensed 98% fat-free cream of chicken soup with 30% less sodium
- ¾ cup shredded Asiago cheese (3 oz)
- ½ cup reduced-fat sour cream
- ½ teaspoon garlic powder
- ½ teaspoon dried rubbed sage
- ¼ teaspoon black pepper

TOPPING

- 2 teaspoons butter
- ⅓ cup crushed oval buttery crackers (10 crackers)
- ¼ cup shredded Asiago cheese (1 oz)
- 1 green onion, chopped

1 In 2-quart saucepan, heat rice and water to boiling, stirring occasionally. Reduce heat to low; cover and cook 40 to 50 minutes or until tender. Drain off excess water.

2 Heat oven to 350°F. Spray 2-quart round or oval casserole with cooking spray. In large bowl, mix remaining casserole ingredients. Stir in rice; spoon into casserole.

3 In small microwavable bowl, microwave butter uncovered on High about 20 seconds or until melted. Stir in crushed crackers; sprinkle over rice mixture.

4 Bake uncovered about 1 hour 10 minutes or until squash is just tender when pierced with fork. (If topping browns too quickly, loosely cover casserole with foil.) Remove from oven. Sprinkle with ¼ cup cheese and the green onion. Let stand 10 minutes before serving.

1 Serving: Calories 500; Total Fat 22g (Saturated Fat 12g, Trans Fat 0.5g); Cholesterol 70mg; Sodium 790mg; Total Carbohydrate 54g (Dietary Fiber 5g); Protein 20g **Exchanges:** 3½ Starch, 1½ High-Fat Meat, 1½ Fat **Carbohydrate Choices:** 3½

make it ahead You can make all or part of this casserole ahead. If you like, cook the wild rice the day ahead, and then mix up the casserole in minutes. Or make the casserole the day ahead and add the topping just before baking.

time-saver Cooking 1 cup wild rice makes about 4 cups cooked rice. If you like, use canned wild rice to shave time from making this casserole.

pepperoni pizza pasta bake

prep time: 10 Minutes || **start to finish:** 50 Minutes || 6 servings (1½ cups each)

4 cups uncooked large elbow macaroni (12 oz)

1 package (5 oz) miniature sliced pepperoni (about 1 cup)

2 cans (18 oz each) fire-roasted tomato cooking sauce

1 can (3.8 oz) sliced ripe olives, drained

1 cup shredded mozzarella cheese (4 oz)

1 Heat oven to 350°F. Cook and drain macaroni as directed on package.

2 In ungreased 3-quart casserole, mix macaroni, pepperoni, cooking sauce and olives.

3 Cover; bake 30 to 35 minutes or until hot in center. Sprinkle with cheese; bake uncovered about 5 minutes longer or until cheese is melted.

1 Serving: Calories 560; Total Fat 18g (Saturated Fat 6g, Trans Fat 0g); Cholesterol 30mg; Sodium 1040mg; Total Carbohydrate 75g (Dietary Fiber 7g); Protein 24g **Exchanges:** 4½ Starch, ½ Other Carbohydrate, 1½ Medium-Fat Meat, 1½ Fat **Carbohydrate Choices:** 5

four-ingredient pizza bake

prep time: 10 Minutes || **start to finish:** 35 Minutes || 8 servings

2 pouches (7.5 oz each)
Bisquick™ Complete
buttermilk biscuit mix

1 cup water

1 jar (14 oz) pizza sauce

1 package (8 oz) sliced
pepperoni

2 cups shredded
mozzarella cheese (8 oz)

1 Heat oven to 375°F. Spray 13x9-inch (3-quart) glass baking dish with cooking spray.

2 In medium bowl, stir Bisquick mix and water until soft dough forms. Drop half of dough by spoonfuls evenly into bottom of baking dish (dough will not completely cover bottom of dish).

3 Drizzle about 1 cup pizza sauce over dough. Arrange half of the pepperoni slices evenly over sauce. Top with 1 cup of the cheese. Repeat layers with remaining dough, pizza sauce, pepperoni and cheese.

4 Bake 20 to 25 minutes or until golden brown. Cut into squares to serve.

1 Serving: Calories 470; Total Fat 28g (Saturated Fat 10g, Trans Fat 45g); Cholesterol 45mg; Sodium 1270mg; Total Carbohydrate 37g (Dietary Fiber 2g); Protein 19g **Exchanges:** 2½ Starch, 1½ High-Fat Meat, 3 Fat **Carbohydrate Choices:** 2½

Quick Variations To make half a recipe, divide the ingredients in half; bake in sprayed 8-inch square (2-quart) glass baking dish 22 to 25 minutes.

Add your favorite pizza toppings to the layers. Try cooked sausage crumbles and chopped green bell pepper, onion or olives.

sausage 'n apple cheddar biscuit bake

prep time: 20 Minutes ‖ **start to finish:** 1 Hour ‖ 12 servings

1 package (1 lb) bulk pork sausage

4 medium cooking apples, coarsely chopped (4 cups)

1 large onion, chopped (1 cup)

6 eggs

1½ teaspoons salt

2¼ cups all-purpose flour

2½ teaspoons baking powder

2 teaspoons sugar

¾ teaspoon baking soda

6 tablespoons cold butter, cut into ½-inch cubes

1½ cups shredded Cheddar cheese (6 oz)

2 medium green onions, finely chopped (2 tablespoons)

1 cup buttermilk

1 Heat oven to 425°F. Spray bottom and sides of 13x9-inch (3-quart) glass baking dish with cooking spray, or grease with shortening.

2 In 12-inch skillet, cook sausage, apples and onion over medium-high heat 8 to 10 minutes, stirring frequently, until sausage is no longer pink; drain if necessary. Spoon into baking dish.

3 In medium bowl, beat eggs and ½ teaspoon of the salt with whisk or fork until well mixed. Pour eggs over sausage mixture.

4 In large bowl, mix flour, baking powder, sugar, baking soda and remaining 1 teaspoon salt. Using pastry blender or fork, cut in butter until mixture looks like coarse crumbs. Stir in cheese and green onions. Add buttermilk; stir just until combined. Drop dough by rounded tablespoonfuls evenly onto sausage mixture.

5 Bake uncovered 20 to 30 minutes or until biscuits are deep golden brown and done in center. Let stand 10 minutes before serving.

1 Serving: Calories 340; Total Fat 19g (Saturated Fat 9g, Trans Fat 0g); Cholesterol 150mg; Sodium 880mg; Total Carbohydrate 28g (Dietary Fiber 2g); Protein 14g **Exchanges:** 1½ Starch, ½ Other Carbohydrate, 1½ Medium-Fat Meat, 2 Fat **Carbohydrate Choices:** 2

Heirloom Recipe and New Twist

italian sausage lasagna

crowd-pleasing

prep time: **1 Hour** || start to finish: **2 Hours** ||
8 servings

- 1 lb bulk Italian sausage or lean (at least 80%) ground beef
- 1 medium onion, chopped (½ cup)
- 1 clove garlic, finely chopped
- 3 tablespoons chopped fresh parsley
- 1 tablespoon chopped fresh or 1 teaspoon dried basil leaves
- 1 teaspoon sugar
- 1 can (15 oz) tomato sauce
- 1 can (14.5 oz) whole tomatoes, undrained
- 8 uncooked lasagna noodles
- 1 container (15 to 16 oz) ricotta cheese or small-curd cottage cheese
- ½ cup grated Parmesan cheese
- 1 tablespoon chopped fresh or 1½ teaspoons dried oregano leaves
- 2 cups shredded mozzarella cheese (8 oz)

1 In 10-inch skillet, cook sausage, onion and garlic over medium heat 8 to 10 minutes, stirring occasionally, until sausage is no longer pink; drain. Stir in 2 tablespoons of the parsley, the basil, sugar, tomato sauce and tomatoes, breaking up tomatoes with a fork. Heat to boiling, stirring occasionally. Reduce heat; simmer uncovered about 45 minutes or until slightly thickened.

2 Heat oven to 350°F. Cook and drain noodles as directed on package. Meanwhile, in small bowl, mix ricotta cheese, ¼ cup of the Parmesan cheese, the oregano and remaining 1 tablespoon parsley.

3 In ungreased 13x9-inch (3-quart) glass baking dish, spread half of the sausage mixture (about 2 cups). Top with 4 noodles. Spread half of the cheese mixture (about 1 cup) over noodles. Sprinkle with half of the mozzarella cheese. Repeat layers, ending with mozzarella. Sprinkle with remaining ¼ cup Parmesan cheese.

4 Cover with foil. Bake 30 minutes. Uncover; bake about 15 minutes longer or until hot and bubbly. Let stand 15 minutes before serving.

1 Serving: Calories 430; Total Fat 23g (Saturated Fat 11g, Trans Fat 0g); Cholesterol 70mg; Sodium 1110mg; Total Carbohydrate 28g (Dietary Fiber 3g); Protein 28g
Exchanges: 2 Starch, 3 Medium-Fat Meat, 1 Fat **Carbohydrate Choices:** 2

ravioli-sausage lasagna

prep time: 20 Minutes ‖ **start to finish:** 9 Hours 35 Minutes ‖ **8 servings**

1¼ lb bulk Italian pork sausage

1 jar (26 to 28 oz) tomato pasta sauce (any variety)

1 bag (25 to 27½ oz) frozen beef, cheese, chicken and herb, sausage or butternut squash–filled ravioli

2½ cups shredded mozzarella cheese (10 oz)

½ cup shredded Asiago or Parmesan cheese (2 oz)

2 tablespoons grated Parmesan cheese

1 In 10-inch skillet, cook sausage over medium heat, stirring occasionally, until no longer pink; drain.

2 In ungreased 13x9-inch (3-quart) glass baking dish, spread ½ cup of the pasta sauce. Arrange single layer of frozen ravioli over sauce; evenly pour 1 cup pasta sauce over ravioli. Sprinkle evenly with 1½ cups sausage, 1 cup of the mozzarella and ¼ cup of the Asiago cheese. Repeat layers with remaining ravioli, pasta sauce and sausage only.

3 Cover tightly with foil; refrigerate at least 8 hours but no longer than 24 hours.

4 Heat oven to 350°F. Bake covered 45 minutes. Remove foil; sprinkle with remaining 1½ cups mozzarella and ¼ cup Asiago cheese and the grated Parmesan cheese. Bake 15 to 20 minutes longer or until cheese is melted and lasagna is hot in center. Let stand 10 minutes before serving.

1 Serving: Calories 440; Total Fat 23g (Saturated Fat 11g, Trans Fat 0g); Cholesterol 65mg; Sodium 870mg; Total Carbohydrate 34g (Dietary Fiber 2g); Protein 25g **Exchanges:** 2 Starch, ½ Other Carbohydrate, 1 Lean Meat, ½ Medium-Fat Meat, 1 High-Fat Meat, 1½ Fat **Carbohydrate Choices:** 2

Quick Variation Stir in 1 can (2¼ ounces) sliced ripe olives, drained, and ¼ cup julienne-cut sun-dried tomatoes in oil and herbs, drained (from 8-ounce jar) into drained sausage in step 1. Continue as directed.

loaded baked potato casserole

prep time: 15 Minutes ‖ **start to finish:** 1 Hour ‖ **8 servings**

1 bag (30 oz) frozen extra-spicy and crispy potato wedges

2 cups chopped cooked ham

8 slices bacon, crisply cooked, crumbled

1 medium bell pepper (any color), chopped (1 cup)

1 cup chopped green onions (about 16 medium)

1 jar (15 oz) cheese dip or process cheese sauce

½ cup sour cream

1 Heat oven to 375°F. Spray 13x9-inch (3-quart) glass baking dish with cooking spray.

2 Arrange potato wedges in baking dish. Bake uncovered 10 to 15 minutes or until thawed and beginning to brown.

3 Top potatoes with half each of the ham, bacon, bell pepper and green onions. Spread cheese dip on top. Sprinkle with remaining ham, bacon and bell pepper.

4 Bake 20 to 30 minutes longer or until cheese dip is melted and potatoes are tender. Top with dollops of sour cream and remaining green onions before serving.

1 Serving: Calories 300; Total Fat 17g (Saturated Fat 8g, Trans Fat 0.5g); Cholesterol 60mg; Sodium 1270mg; Total Carbohydrate 18g (Dietary Fiber 3g); Protein 20g **Exchanges:** ½ Starch, ½ Other Carbohydrate, 2½ Medium-Fat Meat, 1 Fat **Carbohydrate Choices:** 1

healthy twist This "loaded" casserole is great at only 300 calories per serving! But if you want to reduce the calories a little more, use 6 slices bacon and fat-free sour cream.

muffuletta egg bake

prep time: 15 Minutes || start to finish: 1 Hour 5 Minutes || 8 servings

1⅓ cups chopped cooked ham

⅓ cup coarsely chopped pimiento-stuffed green olives

½ cup roasted red bell peppers (from 7-oz jar), drained, chopped

½ loaf (1-lb size) unsliced Italian bread, cut into 1-inch cubes (about 5¼ cups)

8 eggs

2½ cups milk

6 slices (about ¾ oz each) provolone cheese

1 tablespoon shredded Parmesan cheese

1 Heat oven to 350°F. Grease 11x7-inch (2-quart) glass baking dish with butter or cooking spray. In small bowl, mix ham, olives and roasted peppers. In baking dish, toss bread cubes and half of ham mixture.

2 In large bowl, beat eggs and milk with whisk until well blended. Pour over ingredients in baking dish. Top evenly with provolone cheese; sprinkle with remaining ham mixture.

3 Bake uncovered 40 to 45 minutes or until set and edges are golden brown. Sprinkle with Parmesan cheese. Let stand 5 minutes before serving.

1 Serving: Calories 290; Total Fat 15g (Saturated Fat 6g, Trans Fat 0g); Cholesterol 245mg; Sodium 830mg; Total Carbohydrate 17g (Dietary Fiber 1g); Protein 21g **Exchanges:** ½ Starch, ½ Low-Fat Milk, ½ Lean Meat, 1 Medium-Fat Meat, ½ High-Fat Meat, ½ Fat **Carbohydrate Choices:** 1

Quick Variation Italian bread from the bakery or the bread aisle will work for this recipe. Whole wheat bread also works in place of the Italian bread.

bacon, kale and tomato
mac and cheese

prep time: **25 Minutes** ‖ start to finish: **1 Hour** ‖ **6 servings (1⅓ cups each)**

CASSEROLE

  5 slices bacon

  ¼ cup butter

  3 tablespoons all-purpose flour

  1 teaspoon ground mustard

  ½ teaspoon salt

  ⅛ teaspoon pepper

  3 cups milk

  2 cups shredded white sharp Cheddar cheese (8 oz)

 1½ cups uncooked elbow macaroni (6 oz)

  1 cup finely chopped fresh kale or spinach, stems removed (about 7 oz)

  1 can (14.5 oz) fire-roasted diced tomatoes, drained

TOPPING

  1 tablespoon butter

  ½ cup plain panko crispy bread crumbs

1 Heat oven to 375°F. Spray 2-quart casserole with cooking spray. Arrange bacon between sheets of microwavable paper towels on microwavable dinner plate. Microwave on High 3 to 4 minutes or until bacon is crisp. Cool; crumble.

2 In 3-quart saucepan, melt ¼ cup butter over low heat. Stir in flour, mustard, salt and pepper. Cook over medium heat, stirring constantly, until mixture is smooth and bubbly. Remove from heat. Gradually stir in milk. Heat to boiling over medium heat, stirring constantly; boil 1 minute. Stir in cheese, ½ cup at a time, until melted. Remove from heat. Stir in uncooked macaroni. Gently stir in kale, tomatoes and bacon; pour into casserole.

3 Bake uncovered 15 minutes; stir. (If any macaroni is sticking up above surface, press down with back of spoon.) Meanwhile, in small microwavable bowl, microwave 1 tablespoon butter uncovered on High about 40 seconds or until melted. Stir in bread crumbs.

4 Sprinkle topping over macaroni mixture. Bake 12 to 17 minutes longer or until macaroni is tender when pierced with fork and topping is light golden brown. Let stand 5 minutes before serving.

1 Serving: Calories 540; Total Fat 29g (Saturated Fat 17g, Trans Fat 1g); Cholesterol 80mg; Sodium 830mg; Total Carbohydrate 47g (Dietary Fiber 2g); Protein 23g
Exchanges: 3 Starch, ½ Vegetable, 1½ High-Fat Meat, 3 Fat **Carbohydrate Choices:** 3

time-saver We prefer hand-shredded cheese for this recipe because the coating on pre-shredded cheese causes the baked casserole sauce to not be quite as smooth—but in a time crunch, pre-shredded cheese will be just fine.

contemporary tuna-noodle casserole

prep time: 20 Minutes || start to finish: 50 Minutes || 6 servings

2 cups uncooked fusilli pasta (6 oz)

1 jar (16 oz) Alfredo pasta sauce

⅓ cup dry white wine or chicken broth

1 teaspoon dried Italian seasoning

1 teaspoon grated lemon peel

2 cans (5 oz each) solid white albacore tuna in water, drained

1 box (9 oz) frozen sugar snap peas, thawed, drained

1 jar (45 oz) whole mushrooms, drained

½ cup unseasoned dry bread crumbs

2 tablespoons butter, melted

1 Heat oven to 375°F. Spray 11x7-inch (2-quart) glass baking dish or 2-quart casserole with cooking spray. Cook and drain pasta as directed on package, using minimum cook time.

2 In large bowl, stir Alfredo sauce, wine, Italian seasoning, lemon peel, tuna, peas, mushrooms and pasta. Spoon into baking dish.

3 In small bowl, stir together bread crumbs and butter; sprinkle over mixture in baking dish.

4 Bake 25 to 30 minutes or until topping is golden brown.

1 Serving: Calories 530; Total Fat 29g (Saturated Fat 18g, Trans Fat 1g); Cholesterol 100mg; Sodium 730mg; Total Carbohydrate 41g (Dietary Fiber 3g); Protein 24g **Exchanges:** 2½ Starch, 2½ Lean Meat, 4 Fat **Carbohydrate Choices:** 3

Quick Variation This is a great tuna supper, but if you prefer, it's easy to substitute 2 cups cut-up cooked chicken for the tuna.

chunky vegetable lasagna

prep time: **35 Minutes** || start to finish: **1 Hour 25 Minutes** || **8 servings**

12 uncooked lasagna noodles

3 cups small fresh broccoli florets

3 large carrots, coarsely shredded (2 cups)

1 can (14.5 oz) diced tomatoes, drained

1 medium red bell pepper, cut into thin strips

1 medium green bell pepper, cut into thin strips

¾ cup basil pesto

¼ teaspoon salt

1 container (15 oz) ricotta cheese

½ cup grated Parmesan cheese

¼ cup chopped fresh parsley

1 egg

3 tablespoons butter

1 clove garlic, finely chopped

3 tablespoons all-purpose flour

2 cups milk

3 cups shredded mozzarella cheese (12 oz)

1 Heat oven to 350°F. Cook and drain noodles as directed on package.

2 In large bowl, mix broccoli, carrots, tomatoes, bell peppers, pesto and salt. In medium bowl, mix ricotta cheese, Parmesan cheese, parsley and egg.

3 In 2-quart saucepan, melt butter over medium heat. Add garlic; cook about 2 minutes, stirring frequently, until golden. Stir in flour; cook over medium heat, stirring constantly, until mixture is smooth and bubbly. Remove from heat. Stir in milk. Heat to boiling, stirring constantly. Boil and stir 1 minute. Remove from heat.

4 In ungreased 13x9-inch (3-quart) glass baking dish, place 3 noodles. Spread half of the cheese mixture over noodles. Top with 3 noodles and half of the vegetable mixture. Sprinkle with 1 cup of the mozzarella cheese. Top with 3 noodles; spread with remaining cheese mixture. Top with remaining 3 noodles and vegetable mixture. Pour sauce evenly over top. Sprinkle with remaining 2 cups mozzarella cheese.

5 Bake uncovered 35 to 40 minutes or until hot in center. Let stand 10 minutes before serving.

1 Serving: Calories 540; Total Fat 27g (Saturated Fat 11g, Trans Fat 0g); Cholesterol 45mg; Sodium 800mg; Total Carbohydrate 45g (Dietary Fiber 5g); Protein 29g **Exchanges:** 2 Starch, 2 Vegetable, 3 High-Fat Meat, 1 Fat **Carbohydrate Choices:** 3

Quick Variation Frozen broccoli florets, thawed and drained, can be substituted for the fresh broccoli.

roasted-vegetable lasagna with goat cheese

prep time: 25 Minutes || start to finish: 1 Hour 10 Minutes || 8 servings

3 medium bell peppers, cut into 1-inch pieces

3 medium zucchini or yellow summer squash, cut in half lengthwise, then crosswise into ½-inch slices

1 medium onion, cut into 8 wedges, separated into pieces

1 package (8 oz) sliced fresh mushrooms (about 3 cups)

Cooking spray

½ teaspoon salt

¼ teaspoon pepper

12 uncooked lasagna noodles

1 package (5 to 6 oz) chèvre (goat) cheese

1 container (7 oz) refrigerated basil pesto

2 cups tomato pasta sauce

2 cups shredded Italian cheese blend (8 oz)

1 Heat oven to 450°F. Spray 15x10x1-inch pan with cooking spray. In pan, place bell peppers, zucchini, onion and mushrooms in single layer. Spray vegetables with cooking spray; sprinkle with salt and pepper. Roast 15 to 20 minutes, turning vegetables once, until crisp-tender.

2 Meanwhile, cook and drain noodles as directed on package, using minimum cook time. In medium bowl, crumble chèvre cheese into pesto; stir.

3 Spray 13x9-inch (3-quart) glass baking dish with cooking spray. In baking dish, spread ½ cup of the pasta sauce. Top with 3 noodles; spread with half of the pesto mixture and 2 cups of the roasted vegetables. Top with 3 noodles; layer with ¾ cup pasta sauce, 1 cup shredded cheese blend and 2 cups vegetables. Top with 3 noodles; layer with remaining pesto mixture and vegetables. Top with remaining 3 noodles; layer with remaining ¾ cup pasta sauce and 1 cup shredded cheese.

4 Reduce oven temperature to 375°F. Bake 20 to 30 minutes or until hot. Let stand 10 minutes before serving.

1 Serving: Calories 520; Total Fat 26g (Saturated Fat 10g, Trans Fat 0g); Cholesterol 30mg; Sodium 990mg; Total Carbohydrate 47g (Dietary Fiber 5g); Protein 22g **Exchanges:** 1½ Starch, 1 Other Carbohydrate, 2 Vegetable, 2 High-Fat Meat, 2 Fat **Carbohydrate Choices:** 3

artichoke-spinach lasagna

prep time: 20 Minutes ‖ **start to finish:** 1 Hour 30 Minutes ‖ 8 servings

1 medium onion, chopped
(½ cup)

4 cloves garlic, finely
chopped

1 can (14 oz) vegetable
broth

1 tablespoon chopped
fresh or 1 teaspoon dried
rosemary leaves

1 can (14 oz) artichoke
hearts, drained, coarsely
chopped

1 box (9 oz) frozen
chopped spinach,
thawed, squeezed
to drain

1 jar (15 to 17 oz) Alfredo
pasta sauce

9 uncooked lasagna
noodles

3 cups shredded
mozzarella cheese
(12 oz)

1 package (4 oz) crumbled
herb-and-garlic feta
cheese (1 cup)

Fresh rosemary sprigs,
if desired

Lemon wedges,
if desired

1 Heat oven to 350°F. Spray 13x9-inch (3-quart) glass baking dish with cooking spray.

2 Spray 12-inch skillet with cooking spray; heat over medium-high heat. Add onion and garlic; cook about 3 minutes, stirring occasionally, until onion is crisp-tender. Stir in broth and rosemary. Heat to boiling. Stir in artichokes and spinach; reduce heat. Cover; simmer 5 minutes. Stir in pasta sauce.

3 Spread one-fourth of the artichoke mixture in bottom of baking dish. Top with 3 noodles. Sprinkle with ¾ cup of the mozzarella cheese. Repeat layers twice. Spread with remaining artichoke mixture; sprinkle with remaining mozzarella cheese. Sprinkle with feta cheese.

4 Cover with foil. Bake 40 minutes. Uncover; bake about 15 minutes longer or until noodles are tender and lasagna is bubbly. Let stand 10 to 15 minutes before cutting. Garnish with rosemary sprigs and lemon wedges.

1 Serving: Calories 520; Total Fat 31g (Saturated Fat 19g, Trans Fat 1g); Cholesterol 95mg; Sodium 960mg; Total Carbohydrate 35g (Dietary Fiber 7g); Protein 24g **Exchanges:** 2½ Starch, 2 Very Lean Meat, 5½ Fat **Carbohydrate Choices:** 2

Quick Variation Stir in ½ cup chopped pitted kalamata, Greek or ripe olives with the pasta sauce for a Mediterranean version of this recipe.

cheesy rigatoni with eggplant sauce

prep time: **20 Minutes** ‖ start to finish: **50 Minutes** ‖ **4 servings (2 cups each)**

2½ cups uncooked rigatoni pasta (7 oz)

2 tablespoons olive oil

1 medium onion, chopped (½ cup)

1 small eggplant, unpeeled, cut into ½-inch cubes (3 cups)

1 medium zucchini, halved lengthwise, cut into ¼-inch slices (1½ cups)

1 can (14.5 oz) diced tomatoes with basil, garlic and oregano, undrained

1 can (8 oz) tomato sauce

1½ cups shredded mozzarella cheese (6 oz)

1 Heat oven to 350°F. Spray 12x8-inch (2-quart) glass baking dish with cooking spray. Cook and drain pasta as directed on package, using minimum cook time.

2 Meanwhile, in 12-inch nonstick skillet, heat oil over medium-high heat. Add onion, eggplant and zucchini; cook 5 to 7 minutes, stirring frequently, until crisp-tender. Stir in tomatoes and tomato sauce.

3 Spoon cooked pasta into baking dish. Spoon vegetable sauce over pasta.

4 Cover tightly with foil. Bake 20 minutes. Uncover; sprinkle with cheese. Bake uncovered 5 to 7 minutes longer or until cheese is melted.

1 Serving: Calories 540; Total Fat 17g (Saturated Fat 6g, Trans Fat 0g); Cholesterol 25mg; Sodium 1000mg; Total Carbohydrate 71g (Dietary Fiber 8g); Protein 25g **Exchanges:** 4 Starch, 2 Vegetable, 1 Medium-Fat Meat, 2 Fat **Carbohydrate Choices:** 5

make it ahead Put this together the night before you want to serve it. Then, bake it the next night for dinner. Since it will be cold, bake it about 30 minutes before topping with the cheese.

three-cheese spinach and pasta bake

prep time: **20 Minutes** || start to finish: **1 Hour 5 Minutes** || **10 servings**

1 package (7 oz) small pasta shells

1 package (8 oz) sliced fresh mushrooms (about 3 cups)

1 small onion, finely chopped (⅓ cup)

2 boxes (9 oz each) frozen chopped spinach, thawed, squeezed to drain

1 cup Original Bisquick mix

1 cup shredded mozzarella cheese (4 oz)

1 package (4 oz) crumbled tomato-basil feta cheese (1 cup)

⅓ cup grated Parmesan cheese

1 teaspoon salt

½ teaspoon pepper

1¾ cups milk

1 Heat oven to 375°F. Spray 13x9-inch (3-quart) glass baking dish with cooking spray.

2 Cook and drain pasta as directed on package, using minimum cook time. Meanwhile, in 8-inch nonstick skillet, cook mushrooms and onion over medium heat about 5 minutes, stirring frequently, until softened.

3 In large bowl, stir together cooked pasta and thawed spinach. Stir in mushroom mixture. Spread in baking dish. In another bowl, stir remaining ingredients until blended. Pour over pasta mixture.

4 Bake uncovered 35 to 40 minutes or until top is golden brown. Let stand 5 minutes before serving.

1 Serving: Calories 200; Total Fat 9g (Saturated Fat 5g, Trans Fat 0.5g); Cholesterol 25mg; Sodium 700mg; Total Carbohydrate 20g (Dietary Fiber 2g); Protein 11g **Exchanges:** 1 Starch, ½ Low-Fat Milk, ½ Vegetable, 1 Fat **Carbohydrate Choices:** 1

time-saver For extra-speedy prep, use frozen chopped onion. Thaw the spinach quickly in the microwave—1 to 2 minutes will do the trick.

butternut squash–pasta bake

prep time: **25 Minutes** || start to finish: **50 Minutes** || **6 servings**

3 cups uncooked penne pasta (9 oz)

2 packages (12 oz each) frozen butternut squash

1 cup milk

1 cup chicken broth (from 32-oz carton)

2 cups shredded Italian cheese blend (8 oz)

¼ cup butter, cut into pieces

¼ cup pine nuts, toasted*

2 tablespoons chopped fresh sage leaves

½ teaspoon salt

¼ teaspoon pepper

Additional chopped fresh sage, if desired

1 Heat oven to 350°F. Spray 11x7-inch (2-quart) glass baking dish with cooking spray. In 4-quart saucepan, cook pasta as directed on package, using minimum cook time; drain and return to Dutch oven. Spoon into baking dish.

2 Meanwhile, cook squash in microwave as directed on package. In the same 4-quart saucepan, mix cooked squash, milk, broth, 1 cup of the cheese and the butter. Cook over medium heat 4 to 5 minutes, stirring occasionally, until butter and cheese are melted. Remove from heat; stir in pine nuts, 2 tablespoons sage, the salt and pepper.

3 Stir squash mixture into pasta; mix well. Sprinkle with remaining 1 cup cheese. Place baking dish on cookie sheet.

4 Bake uncovered 20 to 25 minutes or until lightly browned and cheese is melted. Garnish with additional sage.

1 Serving: Calories 480; Total Fat 23g (Saturated Fat 12g, Trans Fat 0.5g); Cholesterol 55mg; Sodium 860mg; Total Carbohydrate 50g (Dietary Fiber 5g); Protein 19g **Exchanges:** 3½ Starch, 1 High-Fat Meat, 2½ Fat **Carbohydrate Choices:** 3

*To toast pine nuts, spread in shallow pan. Bake at 350°F for 6 to 10 minutes, stirring occasionally, until light brown.

Quick Variation To make this recipe meatless, use vegetable broth in place of chicken broth.

microwave risotto with winter squash, maple syrup and sage

prep time: 10 Minutes ‖ start to finish: 45 Minutes ‖ 4 servings (1 cup each)

2 tablespoons butter

½ cup finely chopped onion (1 medium)

1 clove garlic, finely chopped

1½ teaspoons salt

¼ teaspoon pepper

1 cup uncooked short-grain Arborio rice

1½ cups vegetable broth

1 cup water

1 box (10 oz) frozen winter squash

¼ cup real maple syrup

½ cup shredded Parmesan cheese (2 oz)

1 tablespoon finely chopped fresh sage leaves

1 In 2-quart microwavable casserole, place butter, onion, garlic, salt and pepper. Cover tightly; microwave on High about 3 minutes or until onion is soft. Add rice; stir to coat with butter. Cover; set aside.

2 In 4-cup microwavable measuring cup, place broth and water. Microwave uncovered 5 minutes or until hot. Pour into rice mixture; stir. Cover tightly; microwave on High 5 minutes or until mixture is boiling.

3 Stir mixture; stir in squash. Cover tightly; microwave on Medium (50%) 12 minutes. Stir; continue to cook on Medium (50%) 5 to 7 minutes longer or until rice is just tender and most of liquid is absorbed.

4 Stir in maple syrup. Top with cheese and sage. Serve immediately.

1 Serving: Calories 370; Total Fat 11g (Saturated Fat 6g, Trans Fat 0g); Cholesterol 25mg; Sodium 1470mg; Total Carbohydrate 58g (Dietary Fiber 3g); Protein 10g **Exchanges:** 2½ Starch, 1½ Other Carbohydrate, 2 Fat **Carbohydrate Choices:** 4

time saver Microwave ovens vary, so know what to look for in the finished dish. Almost all of the liquid should be absorbed and the grains of rice should be tender but not mushy. If your rice needs more time or there's still too much liquid, add a couple more minutes to the microwaving time, being sure to continue microwaving on Medium (50%).

calorie-controlled

black bean and veggie enchiladas

prep time: **25 Minutes** ∥ start to finish: **1 Hour** ∥ **5 servings (2 enchiladas each)**

1 **can (10 oz) green enchilada sauce**

1 **bag (14.4 oz) frozen bell pepper and onion stir-fry**

1 **can (16 oz) refried black beans or traditional refried beans**

½ **teaspoon ground cumin**

½ **teaspoon garlic salt**

1 **package (8.2 oz) flour tortillas for soft tacos and fajitas (6-inch)**

1½ **cups shredded Monterey Jack cheese (6 oz)**

1 Heat oven to 375°F. Spray 13x9-inch (3-quart) glass baking dish with cooking spray. Spread ¼ cup of the enchilada sauce in bottom of dish.

2 Place frozen pepper stir-fry in microwavable pie plate. Cover with microwavable plastic wrap; microwave on High 7 minutes, stirring halfway through cooking. Drain vegetables; pat dry with paper towels. Return vegetables to pie plate. Place uncovered in freezer 5 minutes to cool quickly.

3 Meanwhile, in small bowl, mix refried beans, cumin and garlic salt. Spread each tortilla with slightly less than 3 tablespoons refried bean mixture to within ½ inch of edge.

4 Stir 1 cup of the cheese into vegetable mixture. Spoon about ¼ cup mixture on top of bean mixture on each tortilla. Roll up tortillas; place seam side down in dish. Drizzle with remaining enchilada sauce, entirely covering tortillas.

5 Bake uncovered about 30 minutes or until bubbly and thoroughly heated. Sprinkle with remaining ½ cup cheese; let stand 2 to 3 minutes to melt cheese before serving.

1 Serving: Calories 390; Total Fat 16g (Saturated Fat 7g, Trans Fat 15g); Cholesterol 30mg; Sodium 1320mg; Total Carbohydrate 45g (Dietary Fiber 5g); Protein 17g
Exchanges: 1½ Starch, 1 Other Carbohydrate, 1 Vegetable, ½ Very Lean Meat, 1 High-Fat Meat, 1½ Fat **Carbohydrate Choices:** 3

cheese enchiladas verde

prep time: 15 Minute || start to finish: 40 Minutes || 4 servings (2 enchiladas each)

1½ cups shredded Mexican cheese blend (6 oz)

1 small zucchini, shredded (¾ cup)

¼ cup chopped fresh cilantro

⅓ cup garden vegetable or chives-and-onion cream cheese spread

8 soft corn tortillas (5- or 6-inch)

1 jar (16 oz) green salsa (salsa verde) or green tomatillo salsa (2 cups)

1 medium avocado, pitted, peeled and diced

4 medium green onions, sliced (¼ cup)

1 Heat oven to 350°F. Spray 11x7-inch (2-quart) glass baking dish with cooking spray.

2 In medium bowl, mix shredded cheese, zucchini and cilantro. Spread about 2 teaspoons cream cheese on each tortilla. Top each with about ⅓ cup shredded cheese mixture to within 1 inch of edge. Roll up tortillas; place seam side down in baking dish. Pour salsa over enchiladas.

3 Cover with foil. Bake about 25 minutes or until hot. Top with avocado and onions before serving.

1 Serving: Calories 490; Total Fat 31g (Saturated Fat 15g, Trans Fat 1g); Cholesterol 65mg; Sodium 550mg; Total Carbohydrate 36g (Dietary Fiber 7g); Protein 17g **Exchanges:** ½ Starch, ½ Fruit, ½ Other Carbohydrate, 2½ Vegetable, 1½ Medium-Fat Meat, 4½ Fat **Carbohydrate Choices:** 2½

Quick Variation Regular salsa or picante sauce can be substituted for the green salsa.

moussaka

prep time: 30 Minutes ‖ **start to finish:** 1 Hour 40 Minutes ‖ 4 servings

4 frozen soy-protein burgers or soy-protein vegetable burgers

1 medium eggplant (about 1½ lb), unpeeled, cut into ¼-inch slices

¼ cup all-purpose flour

½ teaspoon salt

½ teaspoon pepper

¼ teaspoon ground nutmeg

¼ teaspoon ground cinnamon

3 cups milk

4 oz (half of 8-oz package) cream cheese, cut into cubes

1 can (15 oz) tomato sauce

2 eggs, beaten

1 Heat oven to 375°F. Grease 3-quart casserole. On large microwavable plate, microwave burgers uncovered on High 2 to 3 minutes, turning once, until thawed. Cut into 1-inch pieces; set aside.

2 In 2-quart saucepan, place eggplant and enough water to cover. Heat to boiling. Cook 5 to 8 minutes or until tender. Drain in colander; set aside.

3 In same saucepan, mix flour, salt, pepper, nutmeg, cinnamon and milk. Heat to boiling, stirring constantly. Boil 1 minute, stirring constantly. Remove from heat. Stir in cream cheese until melted and smooth.

4 Place half of eggplant in casserole. Layer burger pieces, tomato sauce, 1½ cups of the white sauce and remaining eggplant. Stir eggs into remaining white sauce; pour over eggplant.

5 Bake uncovered about 1 hour or until firm. Let stand 10 minutes before serving.

1 Serving: Calories 330; Total Fat 6g (Saturated Fat 25g, Trans Fat 0g); Cholesterol 15mg; Sodium 1560mg; Total Carbohydrate 40g (Dietary Fiber 7g); Protein 29g
Exchanges: 2 Starch, 2 Vegetable, 2½ Very Lean Meat, 1 Fat **Carbohydrate Choices:** 2½

CHAPTER
2

pot pies

easy weeknight chicken pot pie

prep time: **15 Minutes** || start to finish: **1 Hour 5 Minutes** || **6 servings**

1 box refrigerated pie crusts, softened as directed on box

1 can (18 oz) roasted garlic with chicken stock cooking sauce

¼ cup all-purpose flour

½ teaspoon poultry seasoning

½ teaspoon salt

¼ teaspoon pepper

1 bag (12 oz) frozen mixed vegetables

1½ cups chopped cooked chicken

1 Heat oven to 425°F. Make pie crusts as directed on box for two-crust pie, using 9-inch glass pie plate.

2. In 2-quart saucepan, mix together cooking sauce, flour, poultry seasoning, salt and pepper with whisk until smooth. Add vegetables; heat to boiling. Boil 2 minutes, stirring frequently. Stir in chicken. Spoon into crust-lined pie plate.

3 Top with second crust; seal edge and flute. Cut slits in several places in top crust.

4 Bake 30 to 35 minutes or until crust is golden brown. After 15 minutes of baking, cover edge of crust with strips of foil to prevent excessive browning. Let stand 10 minutes before serving. Cut into wedges.

1 Serving: Calories 430; Total Fat 22g (Saturated Fat 8g, Trans Fat 0g); Cholesterol 40mg; Sodium 1020mg; Total Carbohydrate 43g (Dietary Fiber 1g); Protein 14g **Exchanges:** 2½ Starch, ½ Other Carbohydrate, 1 Lean Meat, 3½ Fat **Carbohydrate Choices:** 3

cheesy chicken pot pie

prep time: **20 Minutes** || start to finish: **1 Hour 10 Minutes** || **4 servings**

1 tablespoon vegetable oil

½ cup chopped onion
(1 medium)

½ cup chopped celery
(1 medium stalk)

1 cup thinly sliced carrots
(2 medium)

1 cup frozen cut green
beans, thawed

2 cups chopped cooked
chicken

1 can (10¾ oz) condensed
cream of chicken soup

1 can (10½ oz) chicken
gravy

½ teaspoon dried sage
leaves

1 cup finely shredded
sharp Cheddar cheese
(4 oz)

1 refrigerated pie crust,
softened as directed
on box

1 Heat oven to 375°F. In 10-inch skillet, heat oil over medium-high heat. Add onion and celery; cook 3 to 5 minutes, stirring occasionally, until crisp-tender. Stir in carrots, green beans, chicken, soup, gravy and sage. Cook until bubbly. Stir in ¾ cup of the cheese. Spoon into ungreased deep 2-quart casserole.

2 Place pie crust over hot chicken mixture. Fold over edges to fit inside casserole. Cut small slits in surface of crust with paring knife.

3 Bake 40 minutes. Sprinkle remaining ¼ cup cheese over crust; bake 5 to 6 minutes longer or until crust is deep golden brown and cheese is melted.

1 Serving: Calories 670; Total Fat 41g (Saturated Fat 15g, Trans Fat 0.5g); Cholesterol 105mg; Sodium 1460mg; Total Carbohydrate 44g (Dietary Fiber 3g); Protein 31g **Exchanges:** 1½ Starch, 1 Other Carbohydrate, 1 Vegetable, 3½ Medium-Fat Meat, 4½ Fat **Carbohydrate Choices:** 3

time-saver A food processor makes quick work of slicing veggies. Use the slicing blade to slice the carrots and the metal blade to chop the onion and celery.

gluten-free italian chicken-pesto pot pie

prep time: **10 Minutes** ‖ start to finish: **35 Minutes** ‖ **4 servings**

FILLING

- **2** cups diced cooked chicken
- **1** medium red bell pepper, chopped (1 cup)
- **1** can (14.5 oz) diced tomatoes with basil, garlic and oregano, undrained
- **1** tablespoon Bisquick Gluten Free mix
- **½** teaspoon salt
- **¼** teaspoon pepper

TOPPING

- **1** cup gluten-free shredded Parmesan cheese (4 oz)
- **¾** cup Bisquick Gluten Free mix
- **2** tablespoons gluten-free basil pesto
- **⅓** cup milk
- **1** egg, beaten

1 Heat oven to 350°F. In ungreased 2-quart microwavable casserole, mix filling ingredients. Cover with microwavable plastic wrap. Microwave on High 3 to 4 minutes or until bubbly.

2 In small bowl, stir ½ cup of the cheese and remaining topping ingredients until well blended. Drop mixture by small spoonfuls over chicken mixture. Sprinkle with remaining ½ cup cheese.

3 Bake uncovered 25 minutes or until cheese begins to turn golden brown.

1 Serving: Calories 420; Total Fat 19g (Saturated Fat 8g, Trans Fat 0g); Cholesterol 130mg; Sodium 1330mg; Total Carbohydrate 28g (Dietary Fiber 2g); Protein 35g
Exchanges: 1 Starch, 2 Vegetable, 4 Lean Meat, 1½ Fat **Carbohydrate Choices:** 2

Quick Variation A 7-ounce jar of roasted red bell peppers, drained and chopped, can be substituted for the fresh bell pepper.

healthy twist Always read labels to make sure each recipe ingredient is gluten free. Products and ingredient sources can change.

chicken-mushroom pot pie with sweet potato crust

prep time: 35 Minutes || **start to finish:** 1 Hour 20 Minutes || 6 servings

6 slices bacon

1 medium onion, cut in half lengthwise, then cut into ½-inch wedges

1 large red bell pepper, chopped

2 packages (8 oz each) sliced fresh cremini mushrooms

1 teaspoon dried thyme leaves

¼ cup all-purpose flour

½ cup chicken broth

½ teaspoon salt

3 cups cut-up cooked chicken

2 cups chopped red Swiss chard leaves (stems removed)

1 bag (24 oz) refrigerated mashed sweet potatoes

1 Heat oven to 350°F. Spray 2½-quart casserole with cooking spray. In 12-inch nonstick skillet, cook bacon over medium heat about 10 minutes or until crisp. Transfer from skillet to paper towels; drain and cool. Crumble; set aside.

2 Discard all but 2 tablespoons bacon drippings in skillet. Add onion, bell pepper, mushrooms and thyme to drippings; cook over medium heat about 9 minutes, stirring frequently and breaking apart onion pieces with spoon, until onion is translucent.

3 Sprinkle mushroom mixture with flour; stir until moistened. Stir in broth and salt. Cook about 2 minutes, stirring frequently, until mixture boils and thickens. Stir in chicken; sprinkle with Swiss chard. Cover; cook 2 to 3 minutes or until Swiss chard is partially softened. Remove ¼ cup of the Swiss chard; reserve. Stir bacon into mixture in skillet.

4 Pour chicken-mushroom mixture into casserole. Heat sweet potatoes as directed on bag until 160°F; stir. Swirl reserved Swiss chard into sweet potatoes with spoon. Spoon evenly over mushroom mixture; spread evenly.

5 Bake uncovered about 35 minutes or until filling is hot and potatoes just begin to brown. Cool 5 to 10 minutes before serving.

1 Serving: Calories 320; Total Fat 13g (Saturated Fat 5g, Trans Fat 0g); Cholesterol 75mg; Sodium 860mg; Total Carbohydrate 23g (Dietary Fiber 3g); Protein 27g **Exchanges:** 1 Starch, 1½ Vegetable, 3 Lean Meat, ½ Fat **Carbohydrate Choices:** 1½

cornbread-topped chicken pot pie

prep time: 30 Minutes ‖ start to finish: 1 Hour ‖ 4 servings

1 lb boneless skinless chicken breasts, cut into ½-inch pieces

½ teaspoon peppered seasoned salt

1 large onion, chopped (1 cup)

1 jar (12 oz) chicken gravy

1 bag (1 lb) frozen broccoli, carrots and cauliflower

½ cup sour cream

1 pouch (6.52 oz) cornbread and muffin mix

⅓ cup milk

2 tablespoons butter, melted

1 egg

2 tablespoons shredded Parmesan cheese

1 Heat oven to 400°F. Spray 13x9-inch (3-quart) glass baking dish with cooking spray. Sprinkle chicken with seasoned salt. In 12-inch nonstick skillet, cook chicken and onion over medium-high heat 4 to 6 minutes, stirring occasionally, until chicken is browned.

2 Stir in gravy. Heat to boiling. Reduce heat to medium-low; cover and cook about 5 minutes, stirring occasionally, until chicken is no longer pink in center. Meanwhile, place vegetables in colander. Rinse with hot water until thawed. Remove chicken mixture from heat. Stir in vegetables and sour cream; spoon into baking dish.

3 In medium bowl, mix cornbread mix, milk, butter and egg with spoon just until moistened (batter will be lumpy). Drop batter by spoonfuls into baking dish, around edges of warm chicken mixture. Sprinkle cheese over batter.

4 Bake uncovered 20 to 22 minutes or until cornbread is deep golden brown. Let stand 5 minutes before serving.

1 Serving: Calories 570; Total Fat 24g (Saturated Fat 11g, Trans Fat 0.5g); Cholesterol 160mg; Sodium 1190mg; Total Carbohydrate 53g (Dietary Fiber 4g); Protein 37g **Exchanges:** 2 Starch, 1 Other Carbohydrate, 1 Vegetable, 4 Very Lean Meat, 4 Fat **Carbohydrate Choices:** 3½

Quick Variation This recipe will work with lots of other vegetable combinations. Let your family pick their favorite, or you can substitute leftover cooked vegetables for the frozen vegetables.

gluten-free cheddar biscuit chicken pot pie

prep time: 30 Minutes ∥ **start to finish:** 1 Hour 5 Minutes ∥ 10 servings

POT PIE

- 1 tablespoon olive oil
- 1 medium onion, chopped (½ cup)
- 8 oz white mushrooms, quartered
- 2 carrots, peeled, diced (1 cup)
- 2 teaspoons chopped fresh thyme leaves
- ¼ cup Bisquick Gluten Free mix
- 3 cups reduced-sodium chicken broth (from 32-oz carton)
- 3 cups diced cooked chicken
- 1 cup frozen sweet peas, thawed
- ½ teaspoon salt
- ½ teaspoon pepper

BISCUITS

- 1½ cups Bisquick Gluten Free mix
- ½ cup shredded reduced-fat sharp Cheddar cheese (2 oz)
- ¾ cup milk
- 3 tablespoons butter, softened
- 1 egg

1 Heat oven to 400°F. Grease cookie sheet with shortening or spray with cooking spray.

2 In 5-quart ovenproof Dutch oven, heat oil over medium heat. Add onion; cook about 3 minutes, stirring occasionally, until tender. Add mushrooms, carrots and thyme; cook, stirring occasionally, 3 minutes or until liquid has been extracted from vegetables.

3 Stir in Bisquick mix until vegetables are coated. Stir in broth until Bisquick sauce is smooth. Heat to a simmer; cook until thickened. Stir in chicken, peas, salt and pepper.

4 In large bowl, mix biscuit ingredients. Using spoon, drop dough in 10 mounds onto cookie sheet.

5 Bake pot pie uncovered 20 to 25 minutes or until bubbly, adding biscuits to oven for the last 15 minutes of bake time; bake until golden brown. Let stand 10 minutes before serving. Serve biscuits with pot pie.

1 Serving: Calories 260; Total Fat 10g (Saturated Fat 4.5g, Trans Fat 0g); Cholesterol 70mg; Sodium 670mg; Total Carbohydrate 25g (Dietary Fiber 2g); Protein 18g **Exchanges:** 1 Starch, ½ Other Carbohydrate, ½ Vegetable, 2 Very Lean Meat, 1½ Fat **Carbohydrate Choices:** 1½

healthy twist Always read labels to make sure each recipe ingredient is gluten free. Products and ingredient sources can change.

chicken pot pie with herb crust

prep time: 15 Minutes ‖ **start to finish:** 1 Hour ‖ **8 servings**

4 cups cut-up cooked chicken

1 bag (1 lb) frozen mixed vegetables, thawed

2 cans (10¾ oz each) condensed cream of chicken soup

1 can (10½ oz) condensed chicken broth

2 cups Original Bisquick mix

1½ cups milk

½ teaspoon dried thyme leaves

¼ teaspoon dried sage leaves

Chopped fresh parsley, if desired

1 Heat oven to 350°F. In 4-quart saucepan or Dutch oven, heat chicken, vegetables, soup and broth to boiling, stirring occasionally. Boil and stir 1 minute. Spread in ungreased 13x9-inch (3-quart) glass baking dish.

2 In medium bowl, stir together Bisquick mix, milk, thyme, and sage; pour evenly over soup mixture (crust will rise during baking).

3 Bake uncovered 30 to 40 minutes or until golden brown. Sprinkle with parsley. Let stand 5 minutes before serving.

1 Serving: Calories 380; Total Fat 15g (Saturated Fat 4.5g, Trans Fat 15g); Cholesterol 70mg; Sodium 1240mg; Total Carbohydrate 34g (Dietary Fiber 2g); Protein 28g **Exchanges:** 2 Starch, 3 Lean Meat, 1 Fat **Carbohydrate Choices:** 2

Quick Variation You can use leftover turkey or pork in place of the chicken.

time-saver Use purchased cut-up cooked chicken from the deli, or buy a roasted chicken and cut it up.

healthy twist To reduce the fat to about 10 grams and calories to about 310 per serving, make this recipe using reduced-fat cream of chicken soup, Reduced Fat Bisquick™ mix and fat-free (skim) milk.

chicken stroganoff pot pie

prep time: 20 Minutes || **start to finish:** 5 Hours 30 Minutes || 4 servings

1 package (0.87 to 1.2 oz) dry chicken gravy mix

1 can (10½ oz) condensed chicken broth

1 lb boneless skinless chicken breasts, cut into 1-inch pieces

1 bag (1 lb) frozen stew vegetables, thawed, drained

1 jar (4.5 oz) sliced mushrooms, drained

1 cup frozen sweet peas, thawed, drained

½ cup sour cream

1 tablespoon all-purpose flour

1½ cups Original Bisquick mix

4 medium green onions, chopped (¼ cup)

½ cup milk

1 In 3½- to 6-quart slow cooker, mix dry gravy mix and broth until smooth. Stir in chicken, stew vegetables and mushrooms.

2 Cover; cook on Low heat setting about 4 hours or until chicken is tender.

3 Stir in peas. In a small bowl or cup, mix sour cream and flour; stir into chicken mixture. Cover; cook on High heat setting 20 minutes.

4 In small bowl, stir together Bisquick mix and green onions; stir in milk just until moistened. Drop dough by rounded tablespoonfuls onto hot chicken mixture.

5 Cover; cook on High heat setting 45 to 50 minutes or until toothpick inserted in center of topping comes out clean. Serve immediately.

1 Serving: Calories 510; Total Fat 17g (Saturated Fat 7g, Trans Fat 2g); Cholesterol 90mg; Sodium 1390mg; Total Carbohydrate 53g (Dietary Fiber 4g); Protein 37g **Exchanges:** 3 Starch, 1 Vegetable, 4 Lean Meat, ½ Fat **Carbohydrate Choices:** 3½

Quick Variation You can use a 1-ounce envelope of beef stroganoff mix instead of the chicken gravy mix. The sauce will have slightly more sour cream flavor.

Heirloom Recipe and New Twist

chicken pot pie

prep time: 40 Minutes ‖ start to finish: 1 Hour 15 Minutes ‖ 6 servings

⅓ cup butter

⅓ cup all-purpose flour

⅓ cup chopped onion

½ teaspoon salt

¼ teaspoon pepper

1¾ cups chicken broth

⅔ cup milk

2½ to 3 cups cut-up cooked chicken or turkey

1 box (10 oz) frozen peas and carrots

1 box refrigerated pie crusts, softened as directed on box

1 In 2-quart saucepan, melt butter over medium heat. Stir in flour, onion, salt and pepper. Cook, stirring constantly, until mixture is bubbly; remove from heat. Stir in broth and milk. Heat to boiling, stirring constantly. Boil and stir 1 minute. Stir in chicken and peas and carrots; remove from heat.

2 Heat oven to 425°F. Roll out 1 pie crust into 13-inch square. Ease into ungreased 9-inch square (2-quart) glass baking dish. Pour chicken mixture into crust-lined dish.

3 Roll remaining pie crust into 11-inch square. Cut out designs with 1-inch cookie cutter. Place square over chicken mixture. Arrange cutouts on top crust. Turn edges of pie crust under; flute edge.

4 Bake about 35 minutes or until golden brown.

1 Serving: Calories 670; Total Fat 43g (Saturated Fat 14g, Trans Fat 5g); Cholesterol 80mg; Sodium 1050mg; Total Carbohydrate 44g (Dietary Fiber 3g); Protein 25g **Exchanges:** 3 Starch, 2½ Lean Meat, 6½ Fat **Carbohydrate Choices:** 3

Quick Variations Substitute 1 box (9 ounces) frozen broccoli cuts for the frozen peas and carrots. Stir 1 teaspoon curry powder and a few drops hot pepper sauce into the flour mixture before cooking.

Add 1½ cups sliced baby portabella mushrooms to the flour mixture before cooking in step 1.

cranberry-chicken pot pie

prep time: 30 Minutes || **start to finish:** 1 Hour 5 Minutes || 6 servings

- 1 cup chicken broth (from 32-oz carton)
- 1½ cups cubed (½-inch) dark-orange sweet potato (about 9 oz)
- 1 cup chicken gravy (from 12-oz jar)
- 2 cups fresh baby spinach leaves
- ½ cup sweetened dried cranberries
- 3 cups cut-up cooked chicken
- 1 box refrigerated pie crusts, softened as directed on box
- 1 teaspoon milk

1 Heat oven to 425°F. In 3-quart saucepan, heat broth and sweet potato to boiling. Reduce heat; cover and simmer about 6 minutes or until sweet potatoes are almost tender when pierced with fork. Gently stir in gravy, spinach and cranberries; fold in chicken. Cover; remove from heat.

2 On lightly floured surface, roll out 1 pie crust with rolling pin until 12 inches in diameter. Place crust in ungreased 9- or 10-inch deep-dish pie plate or shallow 2-quart casserole dish; gently press in bottom and up side of pie plate. Do not stretch.

3 Pour chicken mixture into crust-lined pie plate. Top with second crust; seal edge and flute. Brush top crust with milk. Cut several slits in top crust for steam to escape.

4 Bake 25 to 30 minutes or until golden brown. Cool 5 minutes before serving.

1 Serving: Calories 500; Total Fat 24g (Saturated Fat 9g, Trans Fat 0g); Cholesterol 70mg; Sodium 740mg; Total Carbohydrate 50g (Dietary Fiber 2g); Protein 23g **Exchanges:** 2 Starch, 1 Other Carbohydrate, 1 Vegetable, 2 Lean Meat, 3½ Fat **Carbohydrate Choices:** 3

Quick Variation Use cut-up cooked turkey instead of the chicken and leftover sweet potatoes and gravy for another delicious twist on chicken pot pie.

gluten-free impossibly easy chicken club pie

prep time: 10 Minutes ‖ **start to finish:** 45 Minutes ‖ 6 servings

1½ cups diced cooked chicken

¼ cup diced cooked ham

4 slices gluten-free bacon, crisply cooked, crumbled

1 cup gluten-free shredded mozzarella cheese (4 oz)

½ cup Bisquick Gluten Free mix

1 cup milk

3 eggs, beaten

½ cup gluten-free light Caesar dressing

2 cups shredded romaine lettuce

1 cup cherry tomatoes, cut in half

1 Heat oven to 400°F. Spray 9-inch glass pie plate with cooking spray (without flour). In pie plate, layer chicken, ham, bacon and cheese.

2 In medium bowl, stir Bisquick mix, milk, eggs and ¼ cup of the dressing with whisk or fork until blended. Pour over ingredients in pie plate.

3 Bake 25 to 30 minutes or until knife inserted in center comes out clean. Let stand 5 minutes.

4 Meanwhile, in medium bowl, toss lettuce and tomatoes with remaining ¼ cup dressing. Cut pie into wedges; top each wedge with lettuce mixture.

1 Serving: Calories 280; Total Fat 13g (Saturated Fat 5g, Trans Fat 0g); Cholesterol 160mg; Sodium 730mg; Total Carbohydrate 17g (Dietary Fiber 1g); Protein 25g **Exchanges:** ½ Starch, ½ Other Carbohydrate, 3½ Very Lean Meat, 2 Fat **Carbohydrate Choices:** 1

time-saver Save time by purchasing precooked bacon. Read the label to make sure it's gluten-free.

healthy twist Always read labels to make sure each recipe ingredient is gluten free. Products and ingredient sources can change.

calorie-controlled

impossibly easy chicken pot pie

prep time: 5 Minutes || **start to finish: 35 Minutes** || **6 servings**

1⅔ cups frozen mixed vegetables

1 cup cut-up cooked chicken

1 can (10¾ oz) condensed cream of chicken soup

1 cup Original Bisquick mix

½ cup milk

1 egg

1 Heat oven to 400°F. In ungreased 9-inch glass pie plate, mix vegetables, chicken and soup.

2 In small bowl, stir together remaining ingredients with fork until blended. Pour into pie plate.

3 Bake 30 minutes or until golden brown.

1 Serving: Calories 230; Total Fat 9g (Saturated Fat 3g, Trans Fat 1g); Cholesterol 60mg; Sodium 670mg; Total Carbohydrate 25g (Dietary Fiber 3g); Protein 12g **Exchanges:** 1½ Starch, 1 Lean Meat, 1 Fat **Carbohydrate Choices:** 1½

Quick Variation If you like, add a bit of herb flavor by stirring ½ teaspoon of your favorite dried herb into the veggie mixture. Oregano, basil, thyme and dill weed are all great choices.

make it ahead Cover and refrigerate up to 24 hours before baking. You may need to bake a bit longer than the recipe directs since you'll be starting with a cold pie. Watch carefully for doneness.

burrito pot pies

prep time: 25 Minutes || **start to finish:** 45 Minutes || 6 servings

1¼ cups Bisquick Heart Smart™ mix

¾ cup shredded reduced-fat Cheddar cheese (3 oz)

¼ cup water

1 egg

2 cups cut-up cooked chicken

1 jar (16 oz) chunky-style salsa

1 can (15 oz) black beans, drained, rinsed

1 can (11 oz) vacuum-packed whole kernel corn, drained

1 teaspoon ground cumin

1 ripe avocado, pitted, peeled and chopped

Reduced-fat sour cream, if desired

Lime wedges, if desired

1 Heat oven to 400°F. Spray 6 (10-oz) ramekins or custard cups with cooking spray; place in 15x10x1-inch pan.

2 In medium bowl, stir Bisquick mix, ½ cup of the cheese, the water and egg until soft dough forms. Set aside.

3 In 3-quart saucepan, heat chicken, salsa, beans, corn and cumin to boiling. Remove from heat; fold in avocado. Divide chicken mixture evenly among ramekins. Spoon dollop of Bisquick mixture over each (dough will not cover entire top).

4 Bake 15 to 20 minutes or until crust is golden brown and filling is bubbly. Sprinkle with remaining ¼ cup cheese. Serve with sour cream and lime wedges.

1 Serving: Calories 380; Total Fat 12g (Saturated Fat 2.5g, Trans Fat 0g); Cholesterol 80mg; Sodium 1330mg; Total Carbohydrate 42g (Dietary Fiber 5g); Protein 24g **Exchanges:** 2½ Starch, ½ Vegetable, 2 Lean Meat, 1 Fat **Carbohydrate Choices:** 3

Quick Variation Do you have frozen corn on hand? It will work just as well as the canned corn. Just thaw 1¼ cups corn and drain before using.

healthy twist These individual pot pies are the perfect way to help control portions. Ramekins are also ideal for making individual desserts.

turkey-biscuit pot pie

prep time: 25 Minutes || **start to finish:** 55 Minutes || 6 servings

FILLING

- 1 **cup water**
- 2½ **cups ready-to-serve baby-cut carrots (12 oz)**
- 2 **cups cut-up fresh broccoli**
- 3 **tablespoons butter**
- ½ **cup chopped onion (1 medium)**
- 3 **tablespoons all-purpose flour**
- 2 **cups chicken broth (from 32-oz carton)**
- 1 **tablespoon chopped fresh or 1 teaspoon dried sage leaves**
- 2 **cups cubed cooked turkey**

BISCUITS

- 4 **slices bacon**
- 1 **cup Original Bisquick mix**
- ½ **cup milk**
- ½ **cup shredded Cheddar cheese (2 oz)**

1 Heat oven to 400°F. In 2-quart saucepan, heat water to boiling. Add carrots and broccoli; cook about 4 minutes or until carrots and broccoli are crisp-tender. Drain.

2 Meanwhile, in 3-quart saucepan, melt butter over medium heat. Add onion; cook about 2 minutes, stirring occasionally, until tender. Beat in flour with whisk. Gradually beat in broth and sage. Reduce heat to medium-low; cook about 5 minutes, stirring occasionally, until sauce thickens. Stir carrots, broccoli and turkey into sauce. Spoon turkey mixture into ungreased 2-quart casserole.

3 Place bacon on microwavable plate; cover with microwavable paper towel. Microwave on High 4 to 6 minutes or until crisp. Crumble bacon; place in medium bowl. Add remaining biscuit ingredients; stir just until blended. Spoon batter around edge of turkey mixture.

4 Bake uncovered 25 to 30 minutes or until biscuit crust is golden brown.

1 Serving: Calories 360; Total Fat 18g (Saturated Fat 8g, Trans Fat 1g); Cholesterol 75mg; Sodium 900mg; Total Carbohydrate 26g (Dietary Fiber 3g); Protein 23g
Exchanges: 1½ Starch, 1 Vegetable, 2½ Lean Meat, 2 Fat **Carbohydrate Choices:** 2

wild rice–turkey pot pie

prep time: **10 Minutes** ‖ start to finish: **45 Minutes** ‖ **6 servings**

FILLING

- 1 can (15 oz) cooked wild rice, drained
- 2 cups cubed cooked turkey
- 1 bag (1 lb) frozen mixed vegetables, thawed, drained
- 1 can (10¾ oz) condensed 98% fat-free cream of mushroom soup with 30% less sodium
- ¼ cup fat-free (skim) milk
- 2 tablespoons dried minced onion

TOPPING

- 1½ cups Original Bisquick mix
- ¾ cup fat-free (skim) milk
- 1 egg or ¼ cup fat-free egg product

1 Heat oven to 400°F. Reserve ½ cup of the wild rice. In ungreased 2-quart casserole, stir together remaining wild rice and remaining filling ingredients until mixed.

2 In medium bowl, stir reserved ½ cup wild rice and all topping ingredients with whisk or fork just until blended. Pour over turkey mixture.

3 Bake uncovered 25 to 35 minutes or until crust is golden brown.

1 Serving: Calories 440; Total Fat 12g (Saturated Fat 3.5g, Trans Fat 1.5g); Cholesterol 105mg; Sodium 920mg; Total Carbohydrate 52g (Dietary Fiber 6g); Protein 32g **Exchanges:** 3 Starch, 1 Vegetable, 3 Lean Meat **Carbohydrate Choices:** 3½

Quick Variation You can use cooked regular white or brown rice instead of wild rice if you prefer. A 15-ounce can contains about 2 cups wild rice.

beef pot pie with potato biscuit crust

prep time: 20 Minutes || **start to finish:** 55 Minutes || **6 servings**

½ lb cooked deli roast beef, cubed (1½ cups)

2 cups frozen mixed vegetables

1 medium onion, chopped (½ cup)

1 jar (12 oz) beef gravy

⅔ cup dry plain mashed potato mix

⅔ cup hot water

1½ cups Original Bisquick mix

⅓ cup milk

1 tablespoon freeze-dried chopped chives

1 Heat oven to 375°F. In 2-quart saucepan, heat beef, frozen vegetables, onion and gravy to boiling over medium heat, stirring frequently. Boil and stir 1 minute. Keep warm.

2 In medium bowl, stir potato mix and hot water until well mixed; let stand until water is absorbed. Stir in Bisquick mix, milk and chives until dough forms. Place dough on surface sprinkled with Bisquick mix; gently roll in Bisquick mix to coat. Shape dough into a ball; knead 10 times. Pat into 11x7-inch rectangle. Fold dough into thirds.

3 Pour beef mixture into ungreased 11x7-inch (2-quart) glass baking dish. Carefully unfold dough onto beef mixture.

4 Bake 30 to 35 minutes or until crust is golden brown.

1 Serving: Calories 310; Total Fat 11g (Saturated Fat 4g, Trans Fat 1.5g); Cholesterol 25mg; Sodium 740mg; Total Carbohydrate 38g (Dietary Fiber 4g); Protein 15g
Exchanges: 2 Starch, 1 Vegetable, 1 Lean Meat, 1½ Fat **Carbohydrate Choices:** 2½

Quick Variation Use rotisserie chicken from the deli and chicken gravy in place of the beef and beef gravy.

rustic meat and potato pie

prep time: 35 Minutes ‖ **start to finish:** 1 Hour 45 Minutes ‖ 8 servings

1 box refrigerated pie crusts, softened as directed on box

1 lb lean (at least 80%) ground beef

1 tablespoon finely chopped garlic

2 teaspoons vegetable oil

2 cups sliced carrots

2 cups refrigerated cooked diced potatoes with onions (from 20-oz bag)

½ cup cooked real bacon pieces (from 3-oz jar)

¾ teaspoon dried thyme leaves

¾ teaspoon pepper

2 cups beef broth (from 32-oz carton)

5 tablespoons cornstarch

1 egg

1 tablespoon water

1 Heat oven to 425°F. Prepare pie crusts as directed on box for two-crust pie, using 9-inch glass pie plate.

2 In 12-inch skillet, cook beef and garlic over medium-high heat 5 to 7 minutes, stirring occasionally, until beef is thoroughly cooked; drain. Transfer beef mixture to large bowl. In same skillet, heat oil over medium heat. Add carrots; cook 3 to 4 minutes, stirring occasionally, until crisp-tender. Add carrots, potatoes, bacon, thyme and pepper to beef mixture.

3 In small bowl, mix broth and cornstarch with whisk; pour into skillet. Heat to boiling over medium heat. Cook about 2 minutes or until thickened. Pour over beef and vegetables; stir to combine. Spoon mixture into crust-lined pie plate.

4 Top with second crust; seal edge and flute. Cut slits in several places in top crust. In small bowl, beat egg and water. Brush over top crust.

5 Bake 15 minutes. Reduce oven temperature to 375°F; bake 40 to 45 minutes longer or until crust is browned, placing sheet of foil over entire crust for last 20 minutes. Let stand 10 minutes before serving.

1 Serving: Calories 470; Total Fat 25g (Saturated Fat 9g, Trans Fat 1g); Cholesterol 75mg; Sodium 890mg; Total Carbohydrate 45g (Dietary Fiber 2g); Protein 17g
Exchanges: 3 Starch, ½ Vegetable, 1 Medium-Fat Meat, 3½ Fat **Carbohydrate Choices:** 3

bruschetta-topped pasta and meatballs

prep time: 15 Minutes ‖ **start to finish:** 50 Minutes ‖ 8 servings

½ cup refrigerated basil pesto (from 7-oz container)

1 can (15 oz) extra-thick and zesty tomato sauce

2 tablespoons sun-dried tomato paste (from 2.8-oz tube)

¼ teaspoon crushed red pepper flakes

1 cup water

1½ cups uncooked fusilli pasta (about 4½ oz)

26 frozen Italian meatballs (about half of 26-oz bag)

1 cup shredded Parmesan cheese (4 oz)

1 tablespoon butter, softened

2 tablespoons refrigerated basil pesto (from 7-oz container)

8 diagonal slices (½ inch thick) baguette French bread (from 3-inch diameter loaf)

8 to 10 oz cherry or grape tomatoes, cut in half

2 tablespoons shredded Parmesan cheese

1 Heat oven to 350°F. Spray 2-quart microwavable and ovenproof casserole with cooking spray.

2 In casserole, mix ½ cup pesto, the tomato sauce, tomato paste, pepper flakes and water. Cover with microwavable plastic wrap. Microwave on High 3 to 4 minutes or until sauce is hot. Add pasta; stir gently. Stir in meatballs and 1 cup cheese. Push any pasta that sticks up above liquid down into liquid to cover.

3 Bake 25 minutes. Meanwhile, in small cup or bowl, mix butter and 2 tablespoons pesto. Spread mixture on each baguette slice; set aside.

4 Remove casserole from oven. Stir pasta; gently fold in cherry tomatoes. Arrange baguette slices, overlapping if necessary, on pasta mixture to cover most of mixture. Cover loosely with foil; bake 10 minutes.

5 Uncover casserole; sprinkle with 2 tablespoons cheese. Bake about 10 minutes longer or until pasta is fork-tender.

1 Serving: Calories 430; Total Fat 22g (Saturated Fat 8g, Trans Fat 0.5g); Cholesterol 65mg; Sodium 1100mg; Total Carbohydrate 35g (Dietary Fiber 3g); Protein 23g **Exchanges:** 1 Starch, 2 Other Carbohydrate, ½ Lean Meat, 2½ Medium-Fat Meat, 3 Fat **Carbohydrate Choices:** 2

greek spanakopita pie

prep time: 35 Minutes ‖ start to finish: 1 Hour 30 Minutes ‖ 6 servings

1 lb lean (at least 80%) ground beef

1 cup chopped onion (1 large)

1 box (9 oz) frozen chopped spinach, thawed, squeezed to drain

¼ cup chopped fresh Italian (flat-leaf) parsley

½ teaspoon salt

¼ teaspoon pepper

1 can (15 oz) diced tomatoes with Italian-style herbs, undrained

12 sheets frozen phyllo (filo) pastry (14x9 inch), thawed

6 tablespoons butter, melted

¼ cup Italian-style bread crumbs

1 cup crumbled feta cheese (4 oz)

1 Heat oven to 350°F. Spray 9-inch glass pie plate with cooking spray. In 10-inch skillet, cook beef and onion over medium-high heat 5 to 7 minutes, stirring occasionally, until beef is thoroughly cooked; drain.

2 Stir spinach, parsley, salt, pepper and all but ½ cup of the tomatoes into beef mixture. Cook and stir until hot; set aside.

3 Cover phyllo sheets with damp paper towel. Arrange sheets, layering 3 at a time, in an X shape and then in a plus-sign (+) shape to create a spoke pattern on work surface, brushing each with butter and sprinkling with 1 teaspoon of the bread crumbs as it is added. Transfer all layers of phyllo to pie plate, gently easing down sides of pie plate and allowing excess phyllo to hang over edge.

4 Place beef mixture in phyllo; top with cheese. Fold overhanging phyllo up and over filling, leaving 2- to 3-inch center of filling uncovered. Spoon remaining ½ cup tomatoes in center. Brush phyllo with remaining butter.

5 Bake 40 to 50 minutes or until phyllo is golden brown. Let stand 5 minutes before serving.

1 Serving: Calories 400; Total Fat 25g (Saturated Fat 13g, Trans Fat 1.5g); Cholesterol 95mg; Sodium 810mg; Total Carbohydrate 24g (Dietary Fiber 3g); Protein 20g **Exchanges:** 1 Starch, 1 Vegetable, 2 Medium-Fat Meat, 3 Fat **Carbohydrate Choices:** 1½

Quick Variation For a more authentic Greek flavor, substitute ground lamb for the ground beef.

chorizo, white bean and kale pot pie

prep time: **30 Minutes** || start to finish: **1 Hour 15 Minutes** || **6 servings**

12 oz bulk chorizo sausage

2 teaspoons vegetable oil

1 cup shredded carrot

1 medium onion, chopped (½ cup)

2 cloves garlic, finely chopped

¼ cup all-purpose flour

1 cup water

½ cup Alfredo pasta sauce

¼ teaspoon pepper

1 cup finely chopped fresh kale (stems removed)

2 cans (15 oz each) cannellini beans, drained, rinsed

1 bag (24 oz) refrigerated mashed potatoes

3 tablespoons grated Parmesan cheese

1 teaspoon dried Italian seasoning

1 Heat oven to 375°F. Spray 9- or 10-inch deep-dish pie plate or shallow 1½-quart casserole with cooking spray.

2 In 12-inch nonstick skillet, cook sausage over medium-high heat, breaking up with spoon, until browned. Transfer sausage from skillet to paper towels to drain. Wipe skillet clean with paper towel. In same skillet, heat oil over medium heat. Add carrot and onion; cook and stir about 3 minutes or until softened. Add garlic; cook and stir 30 seconds longer.

3 Sprinkle flour over mixture in skillet; stir in until moistened. Stir in water, Alfredo sauce and pepper. Cook over medium-high heat, stirring occasionally, until mixture boils and thickens. Stir in kale. Remove from heat; cover and let stand 3 minutes or until kale is softened. Stir in beans and cooked sausage. Pour into pie plate.

4 Heat potatoes as directed on bag; stir until smooth. Spoon evenly over bean mixture. In small cup or bowl, stir together cheese and Italian seasoning. Sprinkle over potatoes; swirl lightly into potatoes with back of spoon while spreading potatoes evenly over filling.

5 Bake 30 to 35 minutes or until filling is hot and bubbly and potatoes are just beginning to brown. Cool 5 to 10 minutes before serving.

1 Serving: Calories 590; Total Fat 31g (Saturated Fat 13g, Trans Fat 0g); Cholesterol 75mg; Sodium 1250mg; Total Carbohydrate 50g (Dietary Fiber 9g); Protein 28g **Exchanges:** 2 Starch, 1½ Other Carbohydrate, 1 Very Lean Meat, 2 High-Fat Meat, 2½ Fat **Carbohydrate Choices:** 3

italian sausage pot pie with polenta crust

prep time: **20 Minutes** || start to finish: **1 Hour 5 Minutes** || **6 servings**

- 1 lb bulk spicy or sweet Italian pork sausage
- 2 small zucchini, cut in half lengthwise, then crosswise into ¼-inch slices (2½ cups)
- 1 can (16 oz) spicy chili beans in sauce, undrained
- 1 can (14.5 oz) diced tomatoes with garlic and onion, drained
- 1 teaspoon dried basil leaves
- ½ teaspoon dried rosemary leaves, crushed
- 1 cup shredded Italian cheese blend (4 oz)
- 2 eggs
- 1 roll (1 lb) prepared sun-dried tomato polenta

1 Heat oven to 375°F. Spray 2½-quart casserole with cooking spray.

2 In 12-inch nonstick skillet, cook sausage over medium heat about 8 minutes, stirring occasionally, until browned; drain. Add zucchini, beans, tomatoes, basil, rosemary and ¾ cup of the cheese; stir gently. Spoon into casserole.

3 In medium bowl, beat eggs slightly with fork. Crumble polenta into eggs; mix well. Spoon polenta mixture evenly over sausage mixture; spread evenly.

4 Bake uncovered about 25 minutes or until sausage mixture begins to bubble around edges and polenta is firm to the touch.

5 Sprinkle remaining ¼ cup cheese over top; bake about 10 minutes longer or until cheese is melted. Cool 10 minutes before serving.

1 Serving: Calories 340; Total Fat 17g (Saturated Fat 7g, Trans Fat 0g); Cholesterol 110mg; Sodium 1030mg; Total Carbohydrate 27g (Dietary Fiber 4g); Protein 19g
Exchanges: 1½ Starch, 1 Vegetable, ½ Very Lean Meat, 1 High-Fat Meat, 1½ Fat
Carbohydrate Choices: 2

make it ahead You can make the sausage mixture up to a day in advance and spoon it into the casserole; cover and refrigerate up to 24 hours. When ready to bake, uncover and continue as directed, increasing the bake time to about 30 minutes.

ham, broccoli and cheese pot pie

prep time: 15 Minutes || **start to finish:** 50 Minutes || **6 servings**

3½ cups frozen broccoli cuts, thawed, drained

2 cups cut-up cooked ham

2 cans (10¾ oz each) condensed Cheddar cheese soup

¼ cup milk

2 cups Original Bisquick mix

1 cup milk

2 tablespoons yellow mustard

2 eggs

1 Heat oven to 400°F. In ungreased 13x9-inch (3-quart) glass baking dish, mix broccoli, ham, soup and ¼ cup milk.

2 In medium bowl, stir remaining ingredients until blended. Pour over ham mixture.

3 Bake about 35 minutes or until crust is golden brown.

1 Serving: Calories 450; Total Fat 21g (Saturated Fat 8g, Trans Fat 2.5g); Cholesterol 125mg; Sodium 1540mg; Total Carbohydrate 40g (Dietary Fiber 3g); Protein 25g **Exchanges:** 1½ Starch, 1 Other Carbohydrate, 3 Medium-Fat Meat, 1 Fat **Carbohydrate Choices:** 2½

Quick Variation Use 2 cups cut-up cooked chicken or turkey instead of the ham.

cheesy bacon-tomato pie

prep time: 25 Minutes | **start to finish:** 55 Minutes | 6 servings

1 refrigerated pie crust, softened as directed on box

8 slices bacon, cut into ½-inch pieces

1 large sweet onion, chopped (1 cup)

2 medium tomatoes, chopped (1½ cups)

¼ cup chopped fresh basil leaves

¼ cup chopped fresh dill weed

½ cup reduced-fat mayonnaise

3 eggs

¼ teaspoon pepper

1 cup shredded Swiss cheese (4 oz)

1 Heat oven to 450°F. Place pie crust in 9-inch glass pie plate as directed on box for one-crust filled pie. Bake 6 to 7 minutes or until light brown. Cool 15 minutes. Reduce oven temperature to 375°F.

2 Meanwhile, in 10-inch nonstick skillet, cook bacon over medium-high heat about 8 minutes, stirring frequently, until crisp; drain on paper towels. Reserve 1 tablespoon drippings in skillet. Cook onion in bacon drippings over medium heat about 10 minutes, stirring occasionally, until tender and lightly browned.

3 Spoon onion into partially baked crust; sprinkle with tomatoes. Top with basil, dill and bacon. In small bowl, mix mayonnaise, eggs and pepper with whisk. Pour over ingredients in crust. Sprinkle with cheese.

4 Bake 25 to 30 minutes or until light brown and knife inserted in center comes out moist but clean.

1 Serving: Calories 390; Total Fat 27g (Saturated Fat 10g, Trans Fat 0g); Cholesterol 135mg; Sodium 620mg; Total Carbohydrate 23g (Dietary Fiber 1g); Protein 14g **Exchanges:** ½ Starch, ½ Other Carbohydrate, 1 Vegetable, ½ Lean Meat, 1 High-Fat Meat, 3½ Fat **Carbohydrate Choices:** 1½

Quick Variation Other fresh herbs can be used in this recipe. Try tarragon, chives, chervil or mint in addition to the basil and dill.

calorie-controlled

potato-onion-bacon slab pie

prep time: 35 Minutes ‖ **start to finish:** 1 Hour ‖ 6 servings

2 medium Yukon Gold potatoes (¾ lb), peeled, cut into ¼-inch slices

½ lb bacon, cut into ½-inch pieces

1½ cups chopped sweet onions

1 can (8 oz) refrigerated seamless dough sheet

1 cup shredded Gruyère cheese (4 oz)

¼ cup sliced green onions (4 medium)

1 egg

¼ cup whipping cream

½ teaspoon pepper

1 Heat oven to 375°F. Line 15x10x1-inch pan with cooking parchment paper. In medium saucepan, place potatoes and enough water to cover. Heat to boiling. Boil uncovered 5 to 8 minutes or just until tender; drain well.

2 Meanwhile, in 10-inch nonstick skillet, cook bacon over medium-high heat 6 to 8 minutes, stirring frequently, until crisp. Drain on paper towels. Reserve 1 to 2 tablespoons drippings in skillet. Add sweet onions; cook over medium heat about 8 minutes, stirring occasionally, until tender and lightly browned.

3 Remove dough sheet from can; unroll in pan. Gently stretch or roll dough to 14x8-inch rectangle. Leaving 2-inch border around edges, layer potatoes, sweet onions, bacon, ½ cup of the cheese and the green onions on dough. Fold up sides of dough to partially enclose filling, pleating as necessary and pressing to seal.

4 In small bowl, beat egg, whipping cream and pepper with whisk until blended. Slowly pour over filling. Sprinkle with remaining ½ cup cheese.

5 Bake 20 to 25 minutes or until crust is golden brown.

1 Serving: Calories 370; Total Fat 21g (Saturated Fat 10g, Trans Fat 0g); Cholesterol 75mg; Sodium 630mg; Total Carbohydrate 30g (Dietary Fiber 1g); Protein 14g **Exchanges:** 1½ Starch, 1 Vegetable, 1 High-Fat Meat, 2½ Fat **Carbohydrate Choices:** 2

make it ahead To make this pie ahead of time, cook the potatoes, bacon and onions the day before and refrigerate. Assemble the pie up to 2 hours before baking; cover and refrigerate. Add 3 to 5 minutes to the bake time to ensure the filling is hot.

cajun beans and rice pot pie

prep time: 30 Minutes || **start to finish:** 1 Hour 5 Minutes || 6 servings

1½ cups water

¾ cup uncooked regular long-grain white rice

2 stalks celery, chopped

1 medium green bell pepper, chopped

1 medium onion, chopped (½ cup)

1 box refrigerated pie crusts, softened as directed on box

1 can (15 oz) black beans, drained, rinsed

1 can (14.5 oz) diced tomatoes with chipotle chiles, drained

1 can (6 oz) tomato paste

1 tablespoon Cajun seasoning

¼ teaspoon kosher (coarse) salt

¼ teaspoon Cajun seasoning

1 Heat oven to 425°F. In 2-quart saucepan, heat water and rice to boiling. Reduce heat; cover and cook 9 minutes. Stir in celery, bell pepper and onion. Heat to boiling. Reduce heat; cover and cook about 6 minutes longer or until rice is tender and most of water is absorbed. Set aside.

2 On lightly floured surface, roll out 1 pie crust with rolling pin until 12 inches in diameter. Place crust in ungreased 9- or 10-inch deep-dish pie plate; gently press in bottom and up side of pie plate. Do not stretch.

3 In large bowl, mix beans, tomatoes, tomato paste and 1 tablespoon Cajun seasoning. Stir in rice mixture. Spoon into crust-lined pie plate. Top with second pie crust; seal edge and flute.

4 In small cup or bowl, stir together salt and ¼ teaspoon Cajun seasoning. Brush top crust lightly with water; sprinkle evenly with seasoning mixture. Cut several slits in top crust for steam to escape.

5 Bake 30 to 35 minutes or until crust is golden brown.

1 Serving: Calories 500; Total Fat 17g (Saturated Fat 7g, Trans Fat 0g); Cholesterol 10mg; Sodium 1390mg; Total Carbohydrate 77g (Dietary Fiber 8g); Protein 11g **Exchanges:** 2½ Starch, 2 Other Carbohydrate, 2 Vegetable, 3 Fat **Carbohydrate Choices:** 5

healthy twist If you are watching sodium content, just omit the salt and use low-sodium tomato paste when you make the pie.

southwestern pot pie

prep time: **15 Minutes** || start to finish: **55 Minutes** || **4 servings**

- 2 tablespoons vegetable oil
- 1 large onion, chopped (1 cup)
- 2 cups cubed peeled sweet potatoes or butternut squash
- 2 cups chunky-style salsa
- ½ cup water
- ¼ teaspoon ground cinnamon
- 1 can (15 to 16 oz) garbanzo beans (chickpeas), drained, rinsed
- 1 cup frozen whole kernel corn, thawed
- 1 pouch (6.5 oz) cornbread and muffin mix
- ½ cup milk
- 1 tablespoon roasted sunflower nuts, if desired

1 In 4-quart Dutch oven or saucepan, heat 1 tablespoon of the oil over medium-high heat. Add onion; cook about 5 minutes, stirring occasionally, until crisp-tender.

2 Stir in sweet potatoes, salsa, water and cinnamon. Heat to boiling. Reduce heat; cover and simmer 20 to 25 minutes or until potatoes are tender. Stir in beans and corn.

3 In medium bowl, mix cornbread mix, milk and remaining 1 tablespoon oil. Stir in sunflower nuts. Drop batter by large spoonfuls onto vegetable mixture. Cover; simmer about 15 minutes or until toothpick inserted in center of dumplings comes out clean.

1 Serving: Calories 590; Total Fat 16g (Saturated Fat 3g, Trans Fat 0.5g); Cholesterol 0mg; Sodium 1230mg; Total Carbohydrate 94g (Dietary Fiber 15g); Protein 17g **Exchanges:** 5 Starch, 1 Other Carbohydrate, 2½ Fat **Carbohydrate Choices:** 6

Quick Variation If you like black beans, feel free to use them in place of the garbanzo beans.

roasted veggie–puff pastry tart

prep time: **20 Minutes** || start to finish: **1 Hour 30 Minutes** || **6 servings**

10 to 12 small yellow fingerling potatoes (about 7 oz), cut in half lengthwise

4 medium carrots (about 9 oz), cut into 1-inch slices

4 teaspoons olive oil

1 teaspoon kosher (coarse) salt

¼ teaspoon pepper

10 medium Brussels sprouts (about 7 oz), ends trimmed, cut in half lengthwise

1 medium leek, rinsed well, cut in half lengthwise, then crosswise into ½-inch pieces (2 cups)

2 tablespoons water

⅓ cup sugar

1 tablespoon white balsamic vinegar

1 tablespoon chopped fresh oregano leaves

1 tablespoon chopped fresh sage leaves

2 cups shredded fontina cheese (8 oz)

1 sheet frozen puff pastry (from 17.3-oz package), thawed

1 Heat oven to 425°F. Line 13x9-inch (3-quart) glass baking dish with heavy-duty foil. Place potatoes and carrots in dish; toss with 2 teaspoons of the oil. Sprinkle ½ teaspoon of the salt and ⅛ teaspoon of the pepper over vegetables; toss and arrange in single layer in dish. Roast 15 minutes. Add Brussels sprouts and leek to baking dish; toss with remaining 2 teaspoons olive oil, ½ teaspoon salt and ⅛ teaspoon pepper. Spread all vegetables in single layer. Roast 15 to 20 minutes longer or just until tender when pierced with fork. Carefully remove foil and vegetables from dish; set aside.

2 Spray same baking dish with cooking spray. In 2-cup microwavable glass measuring cup, mix water and sugar. Microwave uncovered on High 2 to 3 minutes or just until amber colored. Carefully stir in vinegar (mixture will bubble up). Pour evenly into baking dish; quickly spread over bottom. Sprinkle oregano and sage over sugar-vinegar mixture in baking dish. Arrange vegetables over herbs in dish. Sprinkle evenly with cheese.

3 On lightly floured surface, roll out puff pastry with rolling pin into 13x9-inch rectangle. Place pastry over vegetables, folding edges under to fit if necessary. Pierce pastry all over with fork. Bake 20 to 25 minutes longer or until pastry is golden brown. Remove from oven; cool 10 minutes. Place heatproof serving platter upside down over baking dish. Carefully turn platter and dish over; remove dish. If necessary, replace any vegetables or glaze that stick to dish. Cut into squares.

1 Serving: Calories 530; Total Fat 31g (Saturated Fat 11g, Trans Fat 4.5g); Cholesterol 45mg; Sodium 640mg; Total Carbohydrate 47g (Dietary Fiber 4g); Protein 15g **Exchanges:** 1 Starch, 1½ Other Carbohydrate, 2 Vegetable, 1 High-Fat Meat, 4½ Fat **Carbohydrate Choices:** 3

roasted vegetable–goat cheese crostata

prep time: **30 Minutes** ‖ start to finish: **1 Hour 35 Minutes** ‖ **6 servings**

1¼ cups thinly sliced fingerling potatoes

1¼ cups small fresh cauliflower florets

1 cup coarsely chopped red onion

1 cup coarsely chopped red bell pepper

½ cup diagonally sliced carrots

2 large cloves garlic, finely chopped

4½ teaspoons olive oil

¼ teaspoon salt

¼ teaspoon pepper

1 egg

½ cup whipping cream

2 teaspoons chopped fresh or dried thyme leaves

⅛ teaspoon salt

1 refrigerated pie crust, softened as directed on box

⅓ cup crumbled chèvre (goat) cheese

1 Heat oven to 450°F. In large bowl, toss potatoes, cauliflower, onion, bell pepper, carrots, garlic, oil, ¼ teaspoon salt and ⅛ teaspoon of the pepper. Arrange vegetables in single layer in ungreased 15x10x1-inch pan. Roast uncovered 20 minutes or until tender and lightly browned. Cool to room temperature, about 15 minutes. Reduce oven temperature to 425°F.

2 In small bowl, beat egg, whipping cream, thyme, ⅛ teaspoon salt and remaining ⅛ teaspoon pepper with whisk.

3 Line 15x10x1-inch pan with cooking parchment paper; place pie crust in center of pan. Spoon roasted vegetables in center of crust, leaving 1½-inch border around edge. Fold crust border over filling, pleating crust and pressing gently to seal. Carefully pour cream mixture over vegetables. Sprinkle with cheese.

4 Bake 25 to 30 minutes or until crust is browned and knife inserted in center comes out clean. Let stand 5 minutes before serving.

1 Serving: Calories 340; Total Fat 22g (Saturated Fat 10g, Trans Fat 0g); Cholesterol 70mg; Sodium 400mg; Total Carbohydrate 29g (Dietary Fiber 2g); Protein 6g **Exchanges:** 1 Starch, ½ Other Carbohydrate, 1½ Vegetable, 4½ Fat **Carbohydrate Choices:** 2

Quick Variation You can substitute cubed Yukon Gold potatoes for the fingerlings or try different vegetables such as eggplant, zucchini, mixed colors of bell peppers or sweet yellow onion instead of red (using a total of 5 cups of vegetables). The roasting time may vary, so watch carefully.

portabella and vegetable pot pie

prep time: 40 Minutes || **start to finish:** 1 Hour 20 Minutes || 6 servings

1⅓ cups all-purpose flour

½ teaspoon salt

¼ teaspoon dried thyme leaves

⅓ cup vegetable oil

2 tablespoons cold water

1 tablespoon butter

8 oz baby portabella mushrooms, each cut into fourths (3½ cups)

1½ cups half-and-half

1 package (1.6 oz) garlic-herb sauce mix

1 bag (12 oz) frozen mixed vegetables, thawed

1 teaspoon half-and-half

1 In medium bowl, mix flour, salt, thyme and oil until all flour is moistened. Sprinkle with cold water, 1 tablespoon at a time, tossing with fork until all water is absorbed. Gather pastry into a ball. Place pastry between 2 sheets of waxed paper. With rolling pin, roll into 8½-inch round; set aside, covered with towel.

2 Heat oven to 425°F. In 12-inch skillet, melt butter over medium-high heat. Add mushrooms; cook 5 to 7 minutes, stirring frequently, until mushrooms are tender. Stir in 1½ cups half-and-half and the sauce mix. Heat to boiling over medium-high heat, stirring constantly. Stir in vegetables. Cook 2 to 3 minutes, stirring frequently, until thoroughly heated.

3 Spoon vegetable mixture into ungreased 9½-inch deep-dish pie plate. Remove top waxed paper from crust; cut about 1-inch hole in center of crust. Carefully invert crust over filling; remove remaining waxed paper. Cut small slits in several places in crust. Brush crust with 1 teaspoon half-and-half.

4 Bake 25 to 30 minutes or until crust is golden brown. Let stand 10 minutes before serving.

1 Serving: Calories 390; Total Fat 23g (Saturated Fat 8g, Trans Fat 0g); Cholesterol 30mg; Sodium 710mg; Total Carbohydrate 38g (Dietary Fiber 3g); Protein 8g **Exchanges:** 2 Starch, 1 Vegetable, 4½ Fat **Carbohydrate Choices:** 2½

spinach pizza pie

prep time: **20 Minutes** || start to finish: **1 Hour** || **6 servings**

2 cans (13.8 oz each) refrigerated pizza crust dough

1 can (8 oz) pizza sauce (1 cup)

1 jar (4.5 oz) sliced mushrooms, drained

¼ cup sliced ripe olives

1½ cups shredded mozzarella cheese (6 oz)

2 packages (9 oz each) frozen chopped spinach, thawed, squeezed to drain

1 teaspoon olive or vegetable oil

1 tablespoon grated Parmesan cheese

1 Heat oven to 400°F. Lightly spray 9-inch glass pie plate with cooking spray.

2 Unroll 1 can of pizza crust dough. Place dough in pie plate; press against bottom and side of pie plate to form crust.

3 In small bowl, mix pizza sauce and mushrooms; spoon onto dough in pie plate. Layer with olives, ¾ cup of the mozzarella cheese, the spinach and remaining ¾ cup mozzarella cheese.

4 Unroll remaining can of dough. Press dough into 9-inch round; place over filling. Pinch edges of dough together to seal; roll up edge of dough or flute to form rim. Cut several slits in dough. Brush with oil; sprinkle with Parmesan cheese.

5 Bake 35 to 40 minutes or until deep golden brown. Cut into wedges.

1 Serving: Calories 500; Total Fat 16g (Saturated Fat 5g, Trans Fat 0g); Cholesterol 15mg; Sodium 1150mg; Total Carbohydrate 72g (Dietary Fiber 6g); Protein 20g **Exchanges:** 4½ Starch, 1 Vegetable, ½ Medium-Fat Meat, 2 Fat **Carbohydrate Choices:** 4½

herbed roast chicken and vegetables

prep time: **20 Minutes** || start to finish: **2 Hours 10 Minutes** || **6 servings**

¼ cup olive or vegetable oil

2 tablespoons chopped fresh or 1 teaspoon dried thyme leaves

2 tablespoons chopped fresh or 1 teaspoon dried marjoram leaves

½ teaspoon salt

¼ teaspoon coarse ground black pepper

1 lemon

1 whole chicken (4 to 5 lb)

6 small red potatoes, cut in half

1 cup ready-to-eat baby-cut carrots

8 oz fresh green beans, trimmed

1 Heat oven to 375°F. In small bowl, mix oil, thyme, marjoram, salt and pepper. Grate 1 teaspoon peel from lemon; stir peel into oil mixture. Cut lemon into fourths; place in cavity of chicken.

2 Fold wings across back of chicken so tips are touching. Skewer or tie legs together. On rack in shallow roasting pan or in 13x9-inch pan fitted with rack, place chicken, breast side up. Brush some of the oil mixture on chicken. Insert ovenproof meat thermometer so tip is in thickest part of thigh and does not touch bone.

3 Roast uncovered 45 minutes. Arrange potatoes, carrots and green beans around chicken; brush remaining oil mixture on chicken and vegetables. Roast uncovered 30 to 45 minutes longer or until thermometer reads at least 165°F, legs move easily when lifted or twisted and vegetables are tender. Cover loosely with foil; let stand 15 to 20 minutes for easiest carving.

4 Remove lemon; discard. Place chicken on platter; arrange vegetables around chicken. Serve with pan drippings.

1 Serving: Calories 480; Total Fat 27g (Saturated Fat 6g, Trans Fat 0.5g); Cholesterol 115mg; Sodium 320mg; Total Carbohydrate 23g (Dietary Fiber 4g); Protein 38g **Exchanges:** 1 Starch, 2 Vegetable, 4½ Lean Meat **Carbohydrate Choices:** 1½

provençal roast chicken

prep time: **15 Minutes** || start to finish: **2 Hours 15 Minutes** || **6 servings**

1 **whole chicken (3 to 3½ lb)**

1 **lemon**

1 **teaspoon olive oil**

1 **tablespoon dried herbes de Provence**

¼ **teaspoon pepper**

8 **small red potatoes (1½ lb), cut into fourths**

2 **medium zucchini, cut into 1½-inch pieces**

1 **can (14.5 oz) diced tomatoes with basil, garlic and oregano, drained**

½ **cup chopped pitted kalamata olives**

1 Heat oven to 400°F. Fold wings of chicken across back so tips are touching. Skewer or tie legs together. In shallow roasting pan, place chicken, breast side up.

2 Grate peel from lemon; squeeze juice. In small bowl, mix lemon peel, lemon juice and oil. Drizzle half of lemon mixture over chicken; pat herbes de Provence and pepper on skin of chicken. Place squeezed lemon halves inside chicken cavity.

3 In large bowl, toss potatoes, zucchini, tomatoes, olives and remaining lemon mixture. Arrange vegetables around chicken in roasting pan. Insert ovenproof meat thermometer into chicken so tip is in thickest part of inside thigh and does not touch bone.

4 Bake 1 hour 45 minutes to 2 hours or until thermometer reads at least 165°F, legs move easily when lifted or twisted and vegetables are tender.

1 Serving: Calories 320; Total Fat 9g (Saturated Fat 2.5g, Trans Fat 0g); Cholesterol 85mg; Sodium 290mg; Total Carbohydrate 26g (Dietary Fiber 4g); Protein 31g **Exchanges:** 1½ Starch, 1 Vegetable, 3 Lean Meat **Carbohydrate Choices:** 2

time-saver The peel, or zest, of citrus fruits comes from the outermost layer of skin. It contains pungent, aromatic oils that add intense flavor to foods. To easily remove the colored outer peel (not the white), use a grater, paring knife or vegetable peeler.

thyme-roasted chicken with vegetables

prep time: 25 Minutes ‖ **start to finish:** 2 Hours 10 Minutes ‖ 6 servings

1 whole chicken
(3 to 3½ lb)

6 medium carrots, cut into
1-inch pieces

4 medium stalks celery, cut
into 1-inch pieces

3 large baking potatoes
(russet or Idaho), about
8 oz each, unpeeled, cut
into 1½ pieces

3 medium onions, cut into
wedges

2 tablespoons butter,
melted

1 tablespoon chopped
fresh or 1 teaspoon
dried thyme leaves

1 Heat oven to 375°F. Fold wings of chicken across back so tips are touching. Skewer or tie legs together.

2 In shallow roasting pan, place chicken breast side up. Insert ovenproof meat thermometer so tip is in thickest part of inside thigh and does not touch bone. Roast chicken uncovered 45 minutes.

3 Remove chicken from oven. Arrange carrots, celery, potatoes and onions around chicken. Stir thyme into melted butter; drizzle over chicken and vegetables.

4 Cover chicken and vegetables with foil; roast 45 to 60 minutes longer or until thermometer reads at least 165°F, legs move easily when lifted or twisted and vegetables are tender when pierced with fork.

5 Remove vegetables from pan; cover with foil to keep warm while carving the chicken. On cutting board, place chicken, breast up and with legs to your right if you're right-handed or to the left if left-handed. Remove ties from legs. Carve chicken; serve with vegetables.

1 Serving: Calories 400; Total Fat 17g (Saturated Fat 6g, Trans Fat 0.5g); Cholesterol 95mg; Sodium 180mg; Total Carbohydrate 32g (Dietary Fiber 5g); Protein 30g **Exchanges:** 1 Starch, ½ Other Carbohydrate, 1½ Vegetable, 3½ Lean Meat, 1 Fat **Carbohydrate Choices:** 2

oven-roasted chicken and vegetables

prep time: 10 Minutes ‖ **start to finish:** 35 Minutes ‖ 4 servings

2 cups ready-to-eat baby-cut carrots, cut in half lengthwise

2 cups frozen potato wedges with skins (from 24-oz bag)

1 cup frozen whole green beans

1 cup frozen bell pepper and onion stir-fry (from 1-lb bag)

1 cup grape tomatoes

3 tablespoons olive or vegetable oil

½ teaspoon seasoned salt

1 deli rotisserie chicken (2 lb), cut into pieces

1 Heat oven to 425°F. In large bowl, toss all ingredients except chicken.

2 In 15x10x1-inch pan, arrange chicken and vegetables in single layer.

3 Roast uncovered 20 to 25 minutes or until vegetables are crisp-tender and chicken is hot.

1 Serving: Calories 440; Total Fat 20g (Saturated Fat 4g, Trans Fat 0g); Cholesterol 110mg; Sodium 820mg; Total Carbohydrate 27g (Dietary Fiber 6g); Protein 39g **Exchanges:** 1 Starch, 2 Vegetable, 4½ Lean Meat, 1 Fat **Carbohydrate Choices:** 2

chicken and butternut squash

prep time: **10 Minutes** || start to finish: **50 Minutes** || **4 servings**

- 4 **bone-in chicken breasts (about 2 lb), skin removed**
- 1 **tablespoon olive oil**
- ½ **teaspoon salt**
- ½ **teaspoon pepper**
- 5 **cups cubed (½-inch) peeled butternut squash (2¼ lb)**
- 1 **teaspoon fines herbes or ¼ teaspoon dried Italian seasoning**
- 3 **tablespoons dry white wine or reduced-sodium chicken broth**

1 Heat oven to 450°F. Spray roasting pan with cooking spray. Place chicken in pan. Brush chicken with 1½ teaspoons of the oil; sprinkle with ¼ teaspoon each of the salt and pepper.

2 Place squash in large bowl; drizzle with remaining 1½ teaspoons oil. Sprinkle with fines herbes and remaining ¼ teaspoon each salt and pepper; toss well. Spoon squash around chicken.

3 Roast uncovered 35 to 40 minutes or until juice of chicken is clear when thickest part is cut to bone (at least 165°F). Remove chicken and squash from pan; cover to keep warm.

4 Add wine to pan drippings; heat to boiling over high heat, stirring to loosen browned particles. Reduce heat; cook 2 minutes or until sauce is reduced to ¼ cup.

5 On each of 4 plates, place 1 chicken breast and 1 cup squash. Spoon 1 tablespoon sauce over each chicken breast.

1 Serving: Calories 370; Total Fat 8g (Saturated Fat 2g, Trans Fat 0g); Cholesterol 0mg; Sodium 540mg; Total Carbohydrate 37g (Dietary Fiber 6g); Protein 40g
Exchanges: 2½ Starch, 4 Very Lean Meat, 1 Fat **Carbohydrate Choices:** 2½

orange-maple roast chicken and vegetables

prep time: 20 Minutes ‖ **start to finish:** 1 Hour 35 Minutes ‖ **4 servings**

4 chicken leg quarters (4½ lb)
1 teaspoon salt
1 teaspoon pepper
1 tablespoon vegetable oil
¼ cup real maple syrup
¼ cup chicken broth
2 teaspoons grated orange peel
2 tablespoons orange juice
2 tablespoons bourbon
1 tablespoon Dijon mustard
1½ lb fresh Brussels sprouts, trimmed, cut in half
4 carrots, cut into 2-inch pieces
2 tablespoons butter, cut into pieces
½ cup pecan pieces, toasted*

1 Heat oven to 350°F. Sprinkle chicken with ½ teaspoon each of the salt and pepper. In 12-inch skillet or Dutch oven, heat oil over medium-high heat. Add chicken; cook 2 minutes on each side or until browned. Transfer chicken to large shallow roasting pan.

2 In small bowl, mix syrup, broth, orange peel, orange juice, bourbon, mustard, and remaining ½ teaspoon each salt and pepper. Place Brussels sprouts and carrots around chicken in pan; dot with butter. Drizzle vegetables with ¼ cup of the orange mixture. Brush chicken with ¼ cup orange mixture.

3 Roast uncovered 1 hour 15 minutes, brushing every 20 minutes with orange mixture and stirring vegetables once, or until meat thermometer reads at least 165°F.

4 In 1-quart saucepan, heat remaining orange mixture to boiling. Boil 2 minutes. Serve orange sauce with chicken and vegetables. Sprinkle with pecans.

1 Serving: Calories 750; Total Fat 36g (Saturated Fat 10g, Trans Fat 0.5g); Cholesterol 205mg; Sodium 1050mg; Total Carbohydrate 36g (Dietary Fiber 8g); Protein 71g **Exchanges:** 1½ Starch, 1 Other Carbohydrate, ½ Vegetable, 5 Lean Meat, 4 Medium-Fat Meat **Carbohydrate Choices:** 2½

*To toast pecans, spread in shallow pan. Bake at 350°F for 6 to 10 minutes stirring occasionally until light brown.

sage chicken and potatoes

prep time: **15 Minutes** || start to finish: **1 Hour 15 Minutes** || **4 servings**

4 boneless skinless chicken breasts (about 1¼ lb)

3 medium russet potatoes, unpeeled, cut into ¾-inch pieces (3 cups)

1½ cups ready-to-eat baby-cut carrots

1 jar (12 oz) chicken gravy

2 tablespoons Worcestershire sauce

1 teaspoon dried sage leaves

½ teaspoon garlic-pepper blend

1 Heat oven to 400°F. Spray 13x9-inch (3-quart) glass baking dish with cooking spray.

2 In baking dish, arrange chicken, potatoes and carrots. In small bowl, mix remaining ingredients; pour over chicken and vegetables.

3 Spray sheet of foil with cooking spray; place sprayed side down over baking dish. Bake uncovered 50 to 60 minutes or until vegetables are tender and juice of chicken is clear when center of thickest part is cut (at least 165°F).

1 Serving: Calories 320; Total Fat 9g (Saturated Fat 2.5g, Trans Fat 0g); Cholesterol 75mg; Sodium 680mg; Total Carbohydrate 30g (Dietary Fiber 4g); Protein 31g **Exchanges:** 2 Starch, 3½ Very Lean Meat, 1 Fat **Carbohydrate Choices:** 2

Quick Variations You can use bone-in chicken breasts, but they will take a little longer to bake. Chicken is done when juice is clear when center of thickest part is cut to bone (at least 165°F).

If you don't have garlic-pepper blend, you can substitute ¼ teaspoon each garlic powder and coarse ground black pepper.

zesty roasted chicken and potatoes

prep time: 10 Minutes || start to finish: 45 Minutes || 6 servings

6 boneless skinless chicken breasts (about 1¾ lb)

1 lb small red potatoes, cut into fourths

⅓ cup mayonnaise or salad dressing

3 tablespoons Dijon mustard

2 cloves garlic, finely chopped

½ teaspoon pepper

Chopped fresh chives, if desired

1 Heat oven to 350°F. Spray 15x10x1-inch pan with cooking spray.

2 Place chicken and potatoes in pan. In small bowl, mix remaining ingredients except chives; brush over chicken and potatoes.

3 Roast uncovered 30 to 35 minutes or until potatoes are tender and juice of chicken is clear when center of thickest part is cut (at least 165°F). Sprinkle with chives.

1 Serving: Calories 380; Total Fat 23g (Saturated Fat 5g, Trans Fat 0g); Cholesterol 95mg; Sodium 340mg; Total Carbohydrate 14g (Dietary Fiber 2g); Protein 28g **Exchanges:** 1 Starch, 4 Lean Meat **Carbohydrate Choices:** 1

chicken packets milano

prep time: 10 Minutes | **start to finish:** 35 Minutes | 4 servings

4 **boneless skinless chicken breasts (1 lb)**

¼ **cup reduced-calorie zesty Italian or Italian Parmesan dressing**

4 **slices tomato**

12 **fresh sage leaves or ½ teaspoon ground sage**

1 Heat oven to 450°F. Cut 4 (12x12 inch) sheets of heavy-duty foil. Place 1 chicken breast in center of each. Top each with 1 tablespoon dressing, 1 slice tomato and 3 sage leaves.

2 Bring up 2 sides of foil so edges meet. Seal edges, making tight ½-inch fold; fold again, allowing space for heat circulation and expansion. Place packets on ungreased cookie sheet.

3 Bake 20 to 25 minutes or until juice of chicken is no longer pink when center of thickest pieces are cut and thermometer inserted in center reads at least 165°F. To serve, cut large X across top of each packet; carefully fold back foil.

1 Serving: Calories 160; Total Fat 6g (Saturated Fat 1.5g, Trans Fat 0g); Cholesterol 70mg; Sodium 260mg; Total Carbohydrate 2g (Dietary Fiber 0g); Protein 25g **Exchanges:** 3½ Very Lean Meat, 1 Fat **Carbohydrate Choices:** 0

honey-sriracha chicken packets

prep time: 15 Minutes || start to finish: **50 Minutes** || **4 servings**

½ cup uncooked instant brown rice

½ cup water

1 box (7 oz) frozen sliced carrots, sugar snap peas, black beans and edamame lightly tossed with butter sauce, thawed

4 boneless skinless chicken breasts (1¼ lb)

2 tablespoons honey

2 tablespoons lime juice

1 tablespoon Sriracha sauce

1 tablespoon chopped fresh cilantro

1 Heat oven to 350°F. In small bowl, mix rice and water. Soak 5 minutes; drain. Stir in thawed vegetables.

2 Cut 4 (10x12-inch) sheets of heavy-duty foil. Spray center of one side of each with cooking spray. Spoon one-fourth of the rice mixture onto center of each sheet. Top each with 1 chicken breast.

3 In small bowl, mix honey, lime juice and Sriracha sauce. Spoon evenly over chicken.

4 Bring up 2 sides of foil so edges meet. Seal edges, making tight ½-inch fold; fold again, allowing space for heat circulation and expansion. Fold other sides to seal. Place packets on ungreased cookie sheet.

5 Bake about 30 minutes or until juice of chicken is clear when center of thickest part is cut (at least 165°F). Let stand 5 minutes. Place packets on plates. To serve, cut large X across top of each packet; carefully fold back foil. Sprinkle with cilantro.

1 Serving: Calories 310; Total Fat 6g (Saturated Fat 1.5g, Trans Fat 0g); Cholesterol 75mg; Sodium 280mg; Total Carbohydrate 34g (Dietary Fiber 5g); Protein 31g
Exchanges: 2 Starch, ½ Vegetable, 3½ Very Lean Meat, ½ Fat **Carbohydrate Choices:** 2

Quick Variation To grill, place packets on gas grill over medium-low heat or on charcoal grill over medium-low coals; cover grill. Cook 20 to 30 minutes, rotating packets one half turn after 10 minutes, until juice of chicken is clear when center of thickest part is cut (at least 165°F).

creamy chicken-parmesan dinner packets

prep time: **20 Minutes** || start to finish: **1 Hour 10 Minutes** || **6 servings**

1½ cups uncooked instant brown rice

1½ cups water

18 fresh asparagus spears, cut into 1-inch pieces

¾ cup red bell pepper strips (1x½-inch pieces)

6 boneless skinless chicken breasts (about 2½ lb)

Salt and pepper, if desired

1 can (18 oz) creamy Parmesan basil cooking sauce

½ cup shredded Parmesan cheese (2 oz)

1 Heat oven to 350°F. In medium bowl, mix rice and water. Soak 5 minutes; drain. Stir in asparagus and bell pepper.

2 Cut 6 (12x15-inch) sheets of heavy-duty foil. Spray center of one side of each with cooking spray. Spoon one-sixth of rice mixture (about ¾ cup) onto center of each sheet. Top each with 1 chicken breast. Sprinkle chicken with salt and pepper.

3 Pour about ⅓ cup cooking sauce over each chicken breast. Sprinkle with Parmesan cheese.

4 Bring up 2 sides of foil so edges meet. Seal edges, making tight ½-inch fold; fold again, allowing space for heat circulation and expansion. Fold other sides to seal. Place packets on ungreased cookie sheet.

5 Bake 45 to 50 minutes or until juice of chicken is clear when center of thickest part is cut (at least 165°F). Place packets on plates. To serve, cut large X across top of each packet; carefully fold back foil.

1 Serving: Calories 510; Total Fat 15g (Saturated Fat 5g, Trans Fat 0g); Cholesterol 125mg; Sodium 550mg; Total Carbohydrate 41g (Dietary Fiber 6g); Protein 53g
Exchanges: 2 Starch, 2 Vegetable, 6 Very Lean Meat, 2 Fat **Carbohydrate Choices:** 3

Quick Variation Season the chicken with your favorite dried seasoning mix or pepper blend.

roasted chicken sausage with potatoes and cheese

prep time: 20 Minutes || **start to finish:** 1 Hour 5 Minutes || **4 servings**

3 cups frozen diced hash brown potatoes (from 32-oz bag)

2 large bell peppers (any color), seeded, coarsely chopped

2 tablespoons vegetable oil

1 teaspoon salt

½ teaspoon garlic powder

½ teaspoon onion powder

½ teaspoon paprika

⅛ teaspoon pepper

1 package (12 oz) cooked chicken sausages (any flavor)

⅓ cup finely shredded sharp Cheddar cheese

1 Heat oven to 375°F. Line 15x10x1-inch pan with heavy-duty foil; spray foil with cooking spray.

2 In pan, mix potatoes and bell peppers; toss with oil. Sprinkle with salt, garlic powder, onion powder, paprika and pepper; toss until evenly coated. Spread evenly in pan.

3 Poke tops of sausages with fork; arrange on top of potato mixture. Bake 20 minutes.

4 Stir potato mixture; spread evenly in pan. Rearrange sausages on top. Bake 20 minutes longer or until vegetables are tender and sausages are golden brown on top.

5 Sprinkle cheese over potato mixture and sausages. Bake 1 to 2 minutes longer or until cheese is melted.

1 Serving: Calories 380; Total Fat 16g (Saturated Fat 5g, Trans Fat 0g); Cholesterol 65mg; Sodium 1320mg; Total Carbohydrate 39g (Dietary Fiber 4g); Protein 19g
Exchanges: 2½ Starch, 1 Vegetable, 1½ High-Fat Meat, ½ Fat **Carbohydrate Choices:** 2½

southwestern steak with corn and chiles

prep time: 10 Minutes || start to finish: 30 Minutes || 4 servings

2 tablespoons roasted salted hulled pumpkin seeds (pepitas), finely chopped

2 teaspoons Southwest seasoning blend

½ teaspoon pepper

1 lb boneless beef top sirloin steak (1 inch thick)

4 teaspoons olive oil

4 ears fresh sweet corn, husks removed, cut in half crosswise, or 8 frozen small ears corn

2 large poblano chiles, cut in half lengthwise, stems and seeds removed

1 medium onion, cut into 8 wedges

¼ cup roasted salted hulled pumpkin seeds (pepitas)

1 In small bowl, mix 2 tablespoons chopped pumpkin seeds, 1 teaspoon of the seasoning blend and the pepper. Press mixture into all sides of beef; let stand at room temperature 15 minutes.

2 Meanwhile, set oven control to broil. Line 15x10x1-inch pan with heavy-duty foil; spray foil with cooking spray. In same small bowl, mix oil and remaining 1 teaspoon seasoning blend. Place corn, chiles and onion in pan. Drizzle oil mixture over vegetables; toss until evenly coated. Push vegetables together in single layer around sides of pan. Add beef to center of pan.

3 Broil 4 to 6 inches from heat 10 to 15 minutes for medium doneness (150°F), turning beef and vegetables halfway through cooking time.

4 Slice beef; place on platter. Add vegetables to platter; sprinkle with ¼ cup pumpkin seeds.

1 Serving: Calories 410; Total Fat 16g (Saturated Fat 3.5g, Trans Fat 0g); Cholesterol 80mg; Sodium 170mg; Total Carbohydrate 27g (Dietary Fiber 4g); Protein 39g **Exchanges:** 2 Starch, 4 Lean Meat, ½ High-Fat Meat **Carbohydrate Choices:** 2

make it ahead You can prepare and refrigerate this dinner up to 24 hours in advance. Making it ahead will just allow more of the delicious flavors of the marinade to penetrate the beef and veggies. Then, simply pop it in the oven, adding a few extra minutes to the bake time.

roast beef with orange and thyme

prep time: 15 Minutes || start to finish: 2 Hours || 8 servings

1 boneless beef sirloin tip roast (2 to 2½ lb)

½ cup orange marmalade

1 tablespoon olive or vegetable oil

2 teaspoons Sriracha sauce

1 tablespoon dried thyme leaves

1½ teaspoons kosher (coarse) salt

½ teaspoon coarsely ground pepper

8 small (2-inch) red potatoes (about 1½ lb), cut in half crosswise

1 lb fresh asparagus spears, ends trimmed

1 Heat oven to 325°F. Line 15x10x1-inch pan with heavy-duty foil; spray foil with cooking spray. Place beef in pan. In small bowl, mix marmalade, oil and Sriracha sauce; set aside 3 tablespoons for glazing vegetables. Generously brush some of remaining marmalade mixture over beef. Reserve remaining mixture.

2 Roast beef uncovered 40 minutes, brushing beef occasionally with reserved marmalade mixture. Meanwhile, in another small bowl or cup, mix thyme, salt and pepper. Sprinkle top and sides of beef with 2 teaspoons of the thyme mixture. Place potatoes around beef. Generously brush potatoes with some of the 3 tablespoons marmalade mixture; sprinkle with half of the remaining thyme mixture.

3 Roast 45 to 55 minutes longer or until meat thermometer inserted in thickest part of beef reads 135°F. Place beef on cutting board; cover loosely with foil. Let stand about 10 minutes or until thermometer reads 145°F for medium-rare doneness. (Roast to 160°F for medium doneness.) 4 Increase oven temperature to 425°F. Arrange asparagus in single layer in pan with potatoes. Brush asparagus with the rest of the 3 tablespoons marmalade mixture; sprinkle with remaining thyme mixture. Roast 7 to 10 minutes or until asparagus is crisp-tender.

5 To serve, cut beef across grain into thin slices; arrange on serving platter. Add potatoes and asparagus to platter. Spoon pan drippings over beef.

1 Serving: Calories 310; Total Fat 6g (Saturated Fat 1.5g, Trans Fat 0g); Cholesterol 70mg; Sodium 290mg; Total Carbohydrate 31g (Dietary Fiber 3g); Protein 32g **Exchanges:** 1½ Starch, 2 Vegetable, 2 Very Lean Meat, 1½ Lean Meat **Carbohydrate Choices:** 2

beer-braised short rib dinner

prep time: **15 Minutes** || start to finish: **8 Hours 15 Minutes** || **4 servings**

- 4 bone-in beef short ribs, cut in half (about 3¼ lb), trimmed
- 4 teaspoons applewood rub for meat
- 1 can (6 oz) tomato paste
- 1 bottle (12 oz) pale ale
- 6 medium carrots
- 1 medium leek, finely chopped
- 3 cloves garlic, finely chopped
- ½ teaspoon salt
- ¼ teaspoon pepper
- 3 medium Yukon Gold potatoes (about 1¼ lb), cut lengthwise into sixths

1 Line 15x10x1-inch pan with heavy-duty foil; spray foil with cooking spray. Rub ribs on all sides with applewood rub. Place ribs in pan.

2 In medium bowl, stir together tomato paste and beer with whisk until smooth. Finely chop 1 of the carrots. Stir chopped carrot, leek, garlic, salt and pepper into tomato mixture. Pour over ribs, turning to coat. Cover pan tightly with heavy-duty foil. Refrigerate at least 6 hours or up to 24 hours to marinate, turning ribs occasionally.

3 Heat oven to 400°F. Cut remaining 5 carrots into 2-inch pieces. Remove pan from refrigerator. Place carrot pieces in pan with ribs, turning in marinade to coat. Arrange ribs, fat side up, in marinade. Bake uncovered 1 hour.

4 Reduce oven temperature to 350°F. Turn ribs on side; add potatoes to pan, turning in marinade to coat. Bake 45 to 60 minutes longer, occasionally turning ribs, until ribs and potatoes are tender. (If too much beer mixture evaporates, add a little water to pan.)

1 Serving: Calories 510; Total Fat 20g (Saturated Fat 8g, Trans Fat 1g); Cholesterol 95mg; Sodium 940mg; Total Carbohydrate 51g (Dietary Fiber 7g); Protein 32g **Exchanges**: 1½ Starch, 1½ Other Carbohydrate, 1½ Vegetable, ½ Lean Meat, 3 Medium-Fat Meat, ½ Fat **Carbohydrate Choices:** 3½

time-saver If the beef ribs aren't already cut in half, have the butcher cut them for you. Smaller pieces will cook faster and have more surface area to absorb the wonderful flavors of the rub and marinade.

burger and veggie packets

prep time: **15 Minutes** || start to finish: **55 Minutes** || **4 servings**

1 lb extra-lean (at least 90%) ground beef

1 tablespoon Worcestershire sauce

1½ teaspoons garlic-pepper blend

½ teaspoon onion powder

¼ teaspoon salt

2 cups frozen sugar snap peas, carrots, onions and mushrooms (from 1-lb bag)

32 frozen steak fries (from 28-oz bag)

4 frozen half-ears corn-on-the-cob

1 Heat oven to 450°F. Cut 4 (18x12-inch) sheets of heavy-duty foil.

2 In large bowl, mix beef, Worcestershire sauce, 1 teaspoon garlic-pepper blend, the onion powder and salt. Shape mixture into 4 patties, about ¼ inch thick.

3 Place 1 patty on center of each sheet of foil. Top each with ½ cup vegetables and 8 steak fries. Place 1 piece of corn next to each patty. Divide remaining ½ teaspoon garlic-pepper blend among vegetables.

4 Bring up 2 sides of foil so edges meet. Seal edges, making tight ½-inch fold; fold again, allowing space for heat circulation and expansion. Fold other sides to seal. Place packets on ungreased large cookie sheet.

5 Bake 35 to 40 minutes or until meat thermometer inserted in center of patties reads 160°F. Place packets on plates. To serve, cut large X across top of each packet; carefully fold back foil.

1 Serving: Calories 390; Total Fat 13g (Saturated Fat 4.5g, Trans Fat 1.5g); Cholesterol 70mg; Sodium 270mg; Total Carbohydrate 40g (Dietary Fiber 6g); Protein 26g **Exchanges:** 2 Starch, ½ Other Carbohydrate, 1 Vegetable, 2½ Medium-Fat Meat **Carbohydrate Choices:** 2½

calorie-controlled

roasted pork chops and vegetables

prep time: 20 Minutes || **start to finish:** 1 Hour 20 Minutes || 4 servings

4 pork rib chops, ½ inch thick (1 lb)

2 teaspoons parsley flakes

½ teaspoon dried marjoram leaves

½ teaspoon dried thyme leaves

½ teaspoon garlic salt

¼ teaspoon coarsely ground pepper

Olive oil cooking spray

6 small new potatoes, cut into fourths (3 cups)

4 oz fresh mushrooms, cut in half (1½ cups)

1 medium red bell pepper, cut into 1-inch pieces

1 medium onion, cut into thin wedges

1 medium tomato, cut into 8 wedges

1 Heat oven to 425°F. Spray 15x10x1-inch pan with cooking spray.

2 In small bowl, mix parsley, marjoram, thyme, garlic salt and pepper. Spray both sides of pork chops with cooking spray. Sprinkle with 1 to 1½ teaspoons herb mixture. Place 1 pork chop in each corner of pan.

3 In large bowl, mix potatoes, mushrooms, bell pepper and onion. Spray vegetables 2 or 3 times with cooking spray; stir to coat. Sprinkle with remaining herb mixture; toss to coat. Spread evenly in center of pan.

4 Bake 45 minutes. Turn pork; stir vegetables. Place tomato wedges on vegetables. Bake 10 to 15 minutes longer or until pork is slightly pink when cut near bone and vegetables are tender.

1 Serving: Calories 300; Total Fat 9g (Saturated Fat 3g, Trans Fat 0g); Cholesterol 75mg; Sodium 180mg; Total Carbohydrate 27g (Dietary Fiber 5g); Protein 29g **Exchanges:** 1½ Starch, 1 Vegetable, 3 Lean Meat **Carbohydrate Choices:** 1½

healthy twist If you want more veggies, try adding sliced carrots, zucchini and a variety of bell peppers to the vegetable mixture for a bit of color, texture and flavor.

roasted rosemary pork chops and potatoes

prep time: 20 Minutes || **start to finish:** 1 Hour 5 Minutes || **4 servings**

2 tablespoons Dijon mustard

2 tablespoons olive or vegetable oil

½ teaspoon dried rosemary leaves, crushed

½ teaspoon garlic-pepper blend

½ teaspoon seasoned salt

½ teaspoon paprika

3 Yukon Gold potatoes, cut into 1-inch pieces (about 4 cups)

1 medium red onion, cut into ½-inch-wide wedges

4 bone-in loin pork chops, ½ inch thick

1 Heat oven to 425°F. Spray 15x10x1-inch pan with cooking spray. In large bowl, mix mustard, oil, rosemary, garlic-pepper blend, seasoned salt and paprika. Reserve 1 tablespoon of the mustard mixture.

2 Add potatoes and onion to remaining mustard mixture in bowl; toss to coat. Place vegetables in pan.

3 Roast uncovered 25 minutes. Turn and stir potato mixture. Brush pork chops with reserved 1 tablespoon mustard mixture. Place 1 pork chop in each corner of pan.

4 Roast uncovered 15 to 20 minutes longer or until pork is no longer pink when cut near bone and vegetables are tender.

1 Serving: Calories 360; Total Fat 15g (Saturated Fat 4g, Trans Fat 0g); Cholesterol 65mg; Sodium 410mg; Total Carbohydrate 29g (Dietary Fiber 4g); Protein 27g
Exchanges: 2 Starch, 3 Lean Meat, 1 Fat **Carbohydrate Choices:** 2

cheesy italian pork chops with vegetables

prep time: 10 minutes || **start to finish:** 50 minutes || 4 servings

4 bone-in pork loin chops, ½ inch thick (about 1½ lb)

1 teaspoon dried thyme leaves

½ teaspoon garlic-pepper blend

2 tablespoons olive or vegetable oil

3 medium Yukon Gold potatoes, unpeeled, cut into ½-inch cubes

1 red bell pepper, cut into bite-size strips

⅔ cup shredded Italian cheese blend

1 Heat oven to 425°F. Spray 15x10x1-inch pan with cooking spray. Place pork chops in one half of pan.

2 In large bowl, mix ¾ teaspoon of the thyme, the garlic-pepper blend and oil; lightly brush tops and sides of pork with some of the oil mixture. Add potatoes and bell pepper to remaining oil mixture in bowl; toss to coat. Spread vegetables in other half of pan.

3 Bake uncovered 30 to 35 minutes or until pork is no longer pink in center. Sprinkle cheese and remaining ¼ teaspoon thyme over pork; bake 2 to 3 minutes longer or until cheese is melted.

1 Serving: Calories 440; Total Fat 20g (Saturated Fat 6g, Trans Fat 0g); Cholesterol 85mg; Sodium 210mg; Total Carbohydrate 30g (Dietary Fiber 3g); Protein 35g **Exchanges:** 2 Starch, 4 Lean Meat, 1½ Fat **Carbohydrate Choices:** 2

time-saver Pre-shredded cheese is a definite time-saving product. Look for the Italian cheese blend in the dairy case near other shredded cheese products. Depending on the manufacturer, 5 or 6 cheeses are included in the blend. Either type will work in this recipe.

bacon-wrapped pork tenderloin with harvest vegetables

calorie-controlled

prep time: 20 Minutes **║ start to finish:** 1 Hour **║** 6 servings

GLAZE

- 3 tablespoons real maple syrup
- 1 tablespoon olive oil
- 2 teaspoons Dijon mustard
- 2 cloves garlic, finely chopped
- 1 teaspoon dried marjoram leaves
- ¼ teaspoon salt
- ¼ teaspoon pepper

PORK AND VEGETABLES

- 1 small acorn or buttercup squash, cut in half, seeds removed, each half cut into 3 wedges
- 18 medium Brussels sprouts (about 9 oz), ends trimmed
- 3 slices bacon, cut in half
- 1 package (18.4 oz) original flavor pork tenderloin
- 1 large red bell pepper, cut into 1-inch pieces

1 Heat oven to 425°F. Line 15x10x1-inch pan with heavy-duty foil; spray foil with cooking spray. In small bowl, mix glaze ingredients. Reserve 1 tablespoon for pork; set aside. Place squash and Brussels sprouts in pan; brush cut sides of squash and tops of Brussels sprouts with some of the remaining glaze.

2 Roast vegetables 20 minutes. Meanwhile, microwave bacon between layers of microwavable paper towels on microwavable plate on High 3 to 4 minutes or just until edges begin to brown but are still soft and pliable.

3 Push vegetables to edges of pan; place pork in center of pan. Arrange bacon pieces diagonally over top of pork, pressing bacon over sides. Brush bacon with reserved 1 tablespoon glaze. Turn Brussels sprouts over; add bell pepper to pan. Brush bell pepper and Brussels sprouts with remaining glaze.

4 Roast 20 to 25 minutes longer, stirring Brussels sprouts and bell pepper once during cooking, until meat thermometer inserted into center of pork reads 145°F. Let stand at least 3 minutes before serving. Serve pork with vegetables.

1 Serving: Calories 230; Total Fat 8g (Saturated Fat 2.5g, Trans Fat 0g); Cholesterol 40mg; Sodium 550mg; Total Carbohydrate 22g (Dietary Fiber 4g); Protein 18g **Exchanges:** 1 Starch, 1 Vegetable, 2 Lean Meat, ½ Fat **Carbohydrate Choices:** 1½

roast pork with apples and sweet potatoes

prep time: 15 Minutes ‖ start to finish: 1 Hour 15 Minutes ‖ 6 servings

6 tablespoons butter, melted

¼ cup packed brown sugar

1 tablespoon cider vinegar

1 teaspoon salt

½ teaspoon garlic powder

½ teaspoon pepper

2 medium red cooking apples, sliced (about 2 cups)

2 medium dark-orange sweet potatoes, peeled, thinly sliced (about 2½ cups)

1 medium onion, chopped (½ cup)

2 pork tenderloins (1 lb each)

1 Heat oven to 425°F. In medium bowl, mix butter, brown sugar, vinegar, salt, garlic powder and pepper. Reserve 2 tablespoons of butter mixture. To remaining butter mixture, add apples, sweet potatoes and onion; toss to coat. Arrange apple mixture in ungreased roasting pan or 13x9-inch (3-quart) glass baking dish. Cover tightly with foil; bake 20 minutes.

2 Meanwhile, brush pork with reserved butter mixture. Heat 10-inch nonstick skillet over medium-high heat. Add pork; cook about 3 minutes, turning to brown all sides evenly.

3 Place pork on apple mixture in pan; bake uncovered 30 to 40 minutes or until meat thermometer inserted in center reads 145°F. Let stand at least 3 minutes before serving.

1 Serving: Calories 290; Total Fat 8g (Saturated Fat 3.5g, Trans Fat 0g); Cholesterol 80mg; Sodium 480mg; Total Carbohydrate 27g (Dietary Fiber 3g); Protein 27g **Exchanges:** 1 Starch, 1 Fruit, 4½ Lean Meat, ½ Fat **Carbohydrate Choices:** 2

healthy twist Pork tenderloin is a naturally lower-fat cut of meat. It's very lean and, when combined with other healthful ingredients like apples and sweet potatoes, helps make a great healthful meal.

harvest-time pork roast

prep time: 15 Minutes || start to finish: 1 Hour 40 Minutes || 6 servings

1 boneless pork loin roast
(3 to 3½ lb)

½ cup orange marmalade

3 tablespoons orange juice

2 teaspoons fennel seed,
crushed

1 teaspoon dried thyme
leaves

1 teaspoon dried sage
leaves, crushed

2 medium dark-orange
sweet potatoes, peeled,
cut into 1½-inch pieces

1 lb fresh Brussels sprouts,
cut in half if large

2 teaspoons olive or
vegetable oil

½ teaspoon salt

¼ teaspoon pepper

1 Heat oven to 325°F. On rack in shallow roasting pan, place pork. In small bowl, mix marmalade, orange juice, fennel, thyme and sage. Brush half of marmalade mixture over pork.

2 In large bowl, toss sweet potatoes and Brussels sprouts with oil, salt and pepper. Arrange vegetables around pork. Insert ovenproof meat thermometer so tip is in thickest part of pork. Roast uncovered 1 hour.

3 Brush pork with remaining marmalade mixture; gently stir vegetables to coat with pan juices. Roast about 15 minutes longer or until thermometer reads 145°F and vegetables are tender. Remove from oven; cover pork with foil and let stand at least 3 minutes before serving.

1 Serving: Calories 530; Total Fat 20g (Saturated Fat 6g, Trans Fat 0g); Cholesterol 145mg; Sodium 310mg; Total Carbohydrate 35g (Dietary Fiber 5g); Protein 54g **Exchanges:** 1 Starch, 1 Other Carbohydrate, 1 Vegetable, 7 Lean Meat **Carbohydrate Choices:** 2

time-saver It's easy to prepare the veggies up to a day ahead of time. Then seal them in food-storage plastic bags and refrigerate until it's time to cook.

southwest pork packets

prep time: 15 Minutes || start to finish: 45 Minutes || 4 servings

2 cups uncooked instant rice

1½ cups chicken broth (from 32-oz carton)

1 tablespoon Mexican seasoning

1 can (15.25 oz) whole kernel corn, drained

1 small bell pepper (any color), chopped (½ cup)

4 medium green onions, sliced (¼ cup)

4 boneless pork rib or loin chops, ¾ to 1 inch thick (about 1¼ lb)

2 teaspoons Mexican seasoning

Chunky-style salsa, if desired

1 Heat oven to 450°F. Cut 4 (18x12-inch) sheets of heavy-duty foil. Spray half of one side of each sheet with cooking spray.

2 In large bowl, mix rice, broth and 1 tablespoon Mexican seasoning; let stand about 5 minutes or until broth is absorbed. Stir in corn, bell pepper and green onions.

3 Sprinkle each pork chop with ½ teaspoon Mexican seasoning; place in center of sprayed half of foil. Spoon rice mixture over pork. Fold foil over pork and rice so edges meet. Seal edges, making tight ½-inch fold; fold again. Allow space on sides for circulation and expansion. Place packets on ungreased large cookie sheet.

4 Bake 20 to 25 minutes or until pork is no longer pink and meat thermometer inserted in center reads 145°F. Place packets on plates. To serve, cut large X across top of each packet; carefully fold back foil. Serve with salsa.

1 Serving: Calories 500; Total Fat 12g (Saturated Fat 4g, Trans Fat 0g); Cholesterol 85mg; Sodium 790mg; Total Carbohydrate 61g (Dietary Fiber 3g); Protein 37g **Exchanges:** 3½ Starch, 2 Vegetable, 3 Lean Meat **Carbohydrate Choices:** 4

smoked pork chops with apple and sweet potato

prep time: **20 Minutes** ‖ start to finish: **55 Minutes** ‖ **4 servings**

2 tablespoons vegetable oil

1 teaspoon ground cinnamon

½ teaspoon ground cumin

½ teaspoon ground coriander

1 large dark-orange sweet potato, peeled, cut into ½-inch slices, slices quartered

1 large Granny Smith apple, unpeeled, cut into ½-inch pieces

½ small onion, cut into thin wedges, wedges separated

1 tablespoon packed brown sugar

4 fully cooked smoked boneless pork chops (about 2½ oz each)

1 Heat oven to 425°F. Spray 15x10x1-inch pan with cooking spray. In small bowl, mix oil, cinnamon, cumin and coriander.

2 In large bowl, combine sweet potato, apple and onion. Drizzle with 1 tablespoon of the oil-spice mixture; toss to coat. Spread mixture in pan. Bake 30 minutes.

3 Meanwhile, stir brown sugar into remaining oil-spice mixture (mixture will be thick). Rub mixture over 1 side of each pork chop.

4 Remove pan from oven. With spatula, move vegetable mixture to one side of pan. Place pork, coated side up, in other half of pan.

5 Bake 8 to 10 minutes longer or until pork is thoroughly heated and sweet potato and apple are tender.

1 Serving: Calories 260; Total Fat 12g (Saturated Fat 3g, Trans Fat 0g); Cholesterol 45mg; Sodium 45mg; Total Carbohydrate 22g (Dietary Fiber 3g); Protein 16g **Exchanges:** 1 Starch, ½ Other Carbohydrate, 2 Lean Meat, 1 Fat **Carbohydrate Choices:** 1½

mediterranean breaded salmon with vegetables

prep time: **15 Minutes** || start to finish: **45 Minutes** || **4 servings**

VEGETABLES

- 1 box (9 oz) frozen baby lima beans
- 1 medium eggplant, unpeeled, cut into fourths lengthwise, then crosswise into 1-inch pieces
- 2 tablespoons olive oil
- ¼ teaspoon salt
- ⅛ teaspoon pepper
- ½ cup roasted red bell peppers (from a jar), drained, cut into thin strips
- 1 cup fresh baby spinach leaves

SALMON

- 1¼ lb salmon fillet (1 inch thick)
- 1 teaspoon olive oil
- ⅛ teaspoon salt
- ⅛ teaspoon pepper
- 1 cup plain panko crispy bread crumbs
- 2 tablespoons grated lemon peel
- 1 teaspoon dried oregano leaves
- 1 clove garlic, minced
- 1 tablespoon olive oil

1 Heat oven to 375°F. Line 15x10x1-inch pan with heavy-duty foil; spray foil with cooking spray.

2 If lima beans are frozen in solid block, microwave on High about 1 minute or just long enough to break beans apart. Place beans and eggplant in pan; drizzle with 2 tablespoons oil. Sprinkle with ¼ teaspoon salt and ⅛ teaspoon pepper; toss. Spread in single layer in pan. Bake 15 minutes.

3 Pat salmon dry with paper towels. Remove pan from oven. Push vegetables to sides of pan; place salmon skin side down in center. Brush salmon with 1 teaspoon oil; sprinkle with ⅛ teaspoon each salt and pepper. Arrange vegetables in single layer around salmon. In small bowl, mix remaining ingredients. Press half of mixture, about ½ cup, evenly on salmon. Sprinkle remaining mixture over vegetables.

4 Bake 20 to 30 minutes or until fish flakes easily with fork and vegetables are crisp-tender. (If fish browns too quickly, cover loosely with foil.)

5 Spoon beans and eggplant into large heatproof bowl; cover salmon with foil. Toss vegetables with roasted peppers and spinach. Cover with foil; let stand 2 to 3 minutes or until spinach is slightly wilted. Cut salmon into 4 servings; carefully lift fish from skin with pancake turner to serving plate. Serve salmon with vegetables.

1 Serving: Calories 500; Total Fat 24g (Saturated Fat 4g, Trans Fat 0g); Cholesterol 80mg; Sodium 510mg; Total Carbohydrate 33g (Dietary Fiber 9g); Protein 38g **Exchanges:** 1½ Starch, 2 Vegetable, 4½ Lean Meat, 2 Fat **Carbohydrate Choices:** 2

roasted tilapia and vegetables

prep time: 15 Minutes || **start to finish:** 40 Minutes || **4 servings**

8   oz fresh asparagus spears

2   small zucchini, cut in half lengthwise, then crosswise into ½-inch pieces

1   medium bell pepper (any color), cut into ½-inch strips

1   large onion, cut into ½-inch wedges, separated

2   tablespoons olive oil

2   teaspoons Montreal steak seasoning

4   skinless tilapia or other medium-firm fish fillets (6 oz each)

1   tablespoon butter, melted

½   teaspoon paprika

1 Heat oven to 450°F. Snap off tough ends of asparagus; cut each spear in half.

2 In large bowl, mix asparagus, zucchini, bell pepper, onion and oil. Sprinkle with 1 teaspoon of the steak seasoning; toss to coat. Spread vegetables in ungreased 15x10x1-inch pan. Place on lowest oven rack; bake 5 minutes.

3 Meanwhile, spray 13x9-inch (3-quart) glass baking dish with cooking spray. Pat tilapia fillets dry with paper towels. Brush fish with butter; sprinkle with paprika and remaining 1 teaspoon steak seasoning. Place in baking dish.

4 Place baking dish on middle oven rack; bake fish and vegetables uncovered 17 to 18 minutes or until fish flakes easily with fork and vegetables are tender.

1 Serving: Calories 290; Total Fat 12g (Saturated Fat 3.5g, Trans Fat 0g); Cholesterol 100mg; Sodium 520mg; Total Carbohydrate 10g (Dietary Fiber 3g); Protein 34g **Exchanges:** 2 Vegetable, 4 Lean Meat, ½ Fat **Carbohydrate Choices:** ½

herb-crusted tilapia with lemon potatoes

prep time: **15 Minutes** || start to finish: **40 Minutes** || **2 servings**

1 large potato, unpeeled, cut into ½-inch pieces

2 teaspoons olive oil

¼ teaspoon salt

2 tablespoons all-purpose flour

1 egg

¾ cup plain panko crispy bread crumbs

¾ teaspoon seasoned salt

2 tablespoons butter, melted

2 tilapia fillets (5 to 6 oz each)

1 medium zucchini, cut into ½-inch slices

2 teaspoons chopped fresh thyme leaves

2 teaspoons grated lemon peel

1 Heat oven to 425°F. Spray 15x10x1-inch pan with cooking spray. In medium bowl, toss potato, oil and salt to coat. Spread potato pieces in one half of pan. Bake 15 to 20 minutes or until potato is tender.

2 Meanwhile, place flour on plate. In shallow dish, beat egg with fork. In another shallow dish, mix bread crumbs, seasoned salt and butter. Coat fillets with flour. Dip into egg; coat well with bread crumb mixture.

3 Remove pan from oven. Place fillets in other half of pan. Place zucchini over potatoes; toss to combine.

4 Bake 10 to 12 minutes or until fish flakes easily with fork and vegetables are tender. Sprinkle fish with thyme. Sprinkle vegetables with lemon peel; toss.

1 Serving: Calories 660; Total Fat 23g (Saturated Fat 10g, Trans Fat 0.5g); Cholesterol 210mg; Sodium 1360mg; Total Carbohydrate 71g (Dietary Fiber 6g); Protein 41g **Exchanges:** 4 Starch, 1½ Vegetable, 3½ Very Lean Meat, 4 Fat **Carbohydrate Choices:** 5

lemon and herb salmon packets

prep time: 20 Minutes ‖ **start to finish:** 40 Minutes ‖ **2 servings**

1¼ cups reduced-sodium chicken broth (from 32-oz carton)

1 cup uncooked instant brown rice

½ cup matchstick-cut carrots (from 10-oz bag)

2 salmon fillets (4 to 6 oz each)

½ teaspoon lemon-pepper seasoning

2 tablespoons chopped fresh chives

2 lemon slices (¼ inch thick)

1 Heat oven to 450°F. In 1-quart saucepan, heat broth to boiling over high heat. Stir in rice. Reduce heat to low; cover and simmer 5 minutes or until most of broth is absorbed. Stir in carrots.

2 Meanwhile, cut 2 (18x12-inch) sheets of heavy-duty foil; spray with cooking spray. Place fish fillet on center of each sheet. Sprinkle with lemon-pepper seasoning; top with chives. Arrange lemon slices over fish.

3 Spoon rice mixture around each fish fillet. Bring up 2 sides of foil over fish so edges meet. Seal edges, making tight ½-inch fold; fold again, allowing space for heat circulation and expansion. Fold other sides to seal. Place packets in ungreased 15x10-1-inch pan.

4 Bake 16 to 20 minutes or until fish flakes easily with fork. Place packets on plates. Cut large X across top of each packet; carefully fold back foil.

1 Serving: Calories 380; Total Fat 8g (Saturated Fat 2g, Trans Fat 0g); Cholesterol 75mg; Sodium 540mg; Total Carbohydrate 47g (Dietary Fiber 3g); Protein 31g **Exchanges:** 3 Starch, 3 Very Lean Meat, 1 Fat **Carbohydrate Choices:** 3

dilled tuna steak packets

prep time: 20 Minutes ‖ **start to finish:** 50 Minutes ‖ 4 servings

COUSCOUS

- 1 box (5.8 oz) roasted garlic and olive oil–flavored couscous
- 2 teaspoons olive oil

TUNA

- 4 tuna steaks, ¾ inch thick (6 oz each)
- 2 teaspoons chopped fresh dill
- 1 teaspoon salt
- ½ teaspoon pepper

VEGETABLES

- 1 medium zucchini, cut in half lengthwise, then crosswise into ¼-inch slices
- 1 medium yellow squash, cut in half lengthwise, then crosswise into ¼-inch slices
- 3 plum (Roma) tomatoes, cut lengthwise into fourths
- 4 teaspoons olive oil
- 1 tablespoon chopped fresh dill
- ½ teaspoon salt
- ¼ teaspoon pepper

1 Heat oven to 425°F. Cut 4 (18x12-inch) sheets of heavy-duty foil. Make couscous as directed on box using 2 teaspoons oil; stir. Divide evenly onto center of foil sheets (about ½ cup each).

2 Place 1 tuna steak on top of couscous for each packet. Sprinkle each tuna steak with ½ teaspoon of the dill, ¼ teaspoon of the salt and ⅛ teaspoon of the pepper.

3 In medium bowl, toss vegetables ingredients; divide evenly around couscous.

4 Bring up 2 sides of foil so edges meet. Seal edges, making tight 1-inch fold; fold again, allowing space for heat circulation and expansion. Fold other sides to seal. Place packets in ungreased 15x10x1-inch pan.

5 Bake about 20 minutes or until tuna flakes easily with fork and vegetables are tender. To serve, cut large X across top of each packet; carefully fold back foil to allow steam to escape.

1 Serving: Calories 500; Total Fat 17g (Saturated Fat 3g, Trans Fat 0g); Cholesterol 65mg; Sodium 900mg; Total Carbohydrate 38g (Dietary Fiber 4g); Protein 47g **Exchanges:** 2 Starch, 1½ Vegetable, 5½ Very Lean Meat, 2½ Fat **Carbohydrate Choices:** 2½

make it ahead You can prepare these packets the night before and then simply pop them into the oven after work. Increase the bake time to about 35 minutes since they will be coming right from the refrigerator.

baked fish packets with chinese parsley paste

prep time: 30 Minutes || **start to finish:** 30 Minutes || **4 servings**

FISH

- 8 oz daikon radish, peeled, thinly sliced
- 1 lb fresh asparagus spears, cut into 1-inch pieces
- 4 tablespoons dry sherry or chicken broth
- ½ teaspoon salt
- 1 lb cod, flounder or red snapper fillets, cut into 4 serving pieces

PARSLEY PASTE

- 1 cup fresh cilantro leaves
- 1 cup fresh parsley sprigs
- 1 green onion, cut into 1-inch pieces
- 3 cloves garlic, cut in half
- 2 tablespoons lemon juice
- 1 tablespoon canola oil
- ½ teaspoon grated fresh gingerroot
- ¼ teaspoon grated lemon peel

  Pinch salt, if desired

GARNISH, IF DESIRED

  Pine nuts, toasted*

1 Heat oven to 425°F. Cut 4 (18x12-inch) sheets of heavy-duty foil.

2 Divide radish and asparagus evenly among and on center of each sheet of foil. Sprinkle each with 1 tablespoon of the sherry and ⅛ teaspoon of the salt. Top with fish. Bring up 2 sides of foil so edges meet. Seal edges, making tight ½-inch fold; fold again, allowing space for heat circulation and expansion. Fold other sides to seal. Place packets on ungreased cookie sheet.

3 Bake about 15 minutes or until fish flakes easily with fork.

4 Meanwhile, place parsley paste ingredients in blender. Cover; blend on medium to high speed, stopping blender frequently to scrape sides, until smooth.

5 Place packets on plates. Cut large X across top of each packet; carefully fold back foil. Spoon about 2 tablespoons parsley paste over each serving. Garnish with pine nuts.

1 Serving: Calories 170; Total Fat 5g (Saturated Fat 0.5g, Trans Fat 0g); Cholesterol 60mg; Sodium 410mg; Total Carbohydrate 7g (Dietary Fiber 3g); Protein 24g **Exchanges:** 1½ Vegetable, 3 Very Lean Meat, ½ Fat **Carbohydrate Choices:** ½

* To toast pine nuts, spread in shallow pan. Bake at 350°F for 6 to 10 minutes stirring occasionally until light brown.

skillet chicken thighs with bacon and spinach

prep time: 40 Minutes || **start to finish:** 45 Minutes || **4 servings**

8 boneless skinless chicken thighs (3 to 4 oz each)

3 slices bacon, chopped

2 large carrots, chopped (1½ cups)

2 small onions, sliced

3 cloves garlic, chopped

½ cup chicken broth

1 bag (8 oz) fresh baby spinach leaves (6 cups)

½ teaspoon salt

¼ teaspoon pepper

1 tablespoon chopped fresh or ½ teaspoon dried sage leaves

1 tablespoon grated lemon peel

1 In 12-inch skillet, cook chicken and bacon over medium-high heat 5 minutes, turning chicken once.

2 Stir in carrots, onions, garlic and broth. Cook uncovered 15 to 20 minutes, turning chicken and stirring frequently, until juice of chicken is clear when thickest part is cut (at least 165°F) and vegetables are tender.

3 Remove pan from heat; add spinach, salt and pepper. Stir mixture about 3 minutes or until spinach wilts. Stir in sage and lemon peel until well blended.

1 Serving: Calories 350; Total Fat 16g (Saturated Fat 5g, Trans Fat 0g); Cholesterol 110mg; Sodium 720mg; Total Carbohydrate 11g (Dietary Fiber 3g); Protein 40g **Exchanges:** 1½ Vegetable, 5½ Lean Meat **Carbohydrate Choices:** 1

chicken with pan-roasted cauliflower and orzo

prep time: 10 Minutes ‖ **start to finish:** 20 Minutes ‖ **4 servings (1½ cups each)**

1 tablespoon olive oil

2 cups bite-size fresh cauliflower florets

1½ cups chicken broth (from 32-oz carton)

1¼ lb boneless skinless chicken thighs, cut into bite-size pieces

1 cup uncooked orzo or rosamarina pasta (6 oz)

¼ cup thinly sliced green onions with tops (4 medium)

1 can (14.5 oz) diced tomatoes with basil, garlic and oregano, drained

2 cups packed arugula leaves

½ cup shredded Parmesan cheese (2 oz)

1 In 12-inch nonstick skillet, heat oil over medium heat. Add cauliflower; cook about 5 minutes, stirring occasionally, until light brown.

2 Add broth, chicken, orzo, green onions and tomatoes. Heat to boiling. Reduce heat; cover and simmer 8 to 10 minutes or until chicken is no longer pink in center and orzo is tender. Remove from heat.

3 Stir in arugula. Cover; let stand about 1 minute or until arugula is partially wilted. Sprinkle with cheese before serving.

1 Serving: Calories 380; Total Fat 14g (Saturated Fat 5g, Trans Fat 0g); Cholesterol 55mg; Sodium 780mg; Total Carbohydrate 35g (Dietary Fiber 3g); Protein 28g **Exchanges:** 1½ Starch, 2 Vegetable, ½ Lean Meat, 2½ Medium-Fat Meat **Carbohydrate Choices:** 2

Quick Variation Prefer white meat chicken to dark? You can substitute bite-size pieces of boneless skinless chicken breast for the chicken thighs. If you have fresh baby spinach leaves on hand, go ahead and substitute them for the arugula.

calorie-controlled

cheesy chicken skillet dinner

prep time: 20 Minutes || **start to finish:** 20 Minutes || 6 servings

1 teaspoon vegetable oil

1¼ lb boneless skinless chicken breasts, cut into ¾-inch pieces

2 large carrots, cut into ⅛-inch slices (2 cups)

1 medium zucchini, cut into ⅛-inch slices (2 cups)

2 tablespoons soy sauce

8 medium green onions, sliced (½ cup)

2 cups shredded reduced-fat sharp Cheddar cheese (8 oz)

1 Heat 12-inch nonstick skillet over medium-high heat. Add oil; tilt skillet to coat bottom. Add chicken; cook 4 to 5 minutes or until no longer pink in center, stirring frequently. Remove from skillet; cover to keep warm.

2 In same skillet, cook carrots and zucchini 5 minutes or until crisp-tender, stirring frequently. Add chicken and soy sauce; toss until chicken and vegetables are coated with soy sauce. Remove from heat.

3 Sprinkle with green onions and cheese. Cover; let stand 2 minutes to melt cheese.

1 Serving: Calories 210; Total Fat 7g (Saturated Fat 2.5g, Trans Fat 0g); Cholesterol 65mg; Sodium 730mg; Total Carbohydrate 6g (Dietary Fiber 1g); Protein 31g **Exchanges:** ½ Other Carbohydrate, 3½ Lean Meat **Carbohydrate Choices:** ½

Quick Variation Change the flavor and substitute an Italian cheese blend for the Cheddar cheese.

easy chicken with tomatoes and spinach

prep time: **35 Minutes** ‖ start to finish: **35 Minutes** ‖ **4 servings**

1 **tablespoon olive or vegetable oil**

4 **boneless skinless chicken breasts (about 1¼ lb)**

1 **clove garlic, finely chopped**

½ **teaspoon dried oregano leaves**

½ **teaspoon seasoned salt**

¼ **teaspoon pepper**

¼ **cup dry white wine or water**

2 **medium plum (Roma) tomatoes, sliced (about 1 cup)**

1 **bag (6 oz) fresh baby spinach leaves (about 3½ cups)**

1 In 12-inch nonstick skillet, heat oil over medium heat. Sprinkle chicken with garlic, oregano, seasoned salt and pepper. Add chicken to skillet; cook 15 to 20 minutes, turning once, or until juice of chicken is clear when center of thickest part is cut (at least 165°F).

2 Stir wine into skillet. Top chicken with tomato slices. Cover; cook 2 to 3 minutes longer or until tomatoes are thoroughly heated.

3 Add spinach. Cover; cook 2 to 3 minutes longer or until spinach is wilted.

1 Serving: Calories 230; Total Fat 8g (Saturated Fat 2g, Trans Fat 0g); Cholesterol 90mg; Sodium 270mg; Total Carbohydrate 3g (Dietary Fiber 1g); Protein 33g **Exchanges:** ½ Vegetable, 2 Very Lean Meat, 2½ Lean Meat **Carbohydrate Choices:** 0

chicken and orzo supper

prep time: 35 Minutes || **start to finish:** 35 Minutes || 4 servings (1 cup each)

1 tablespoon vegetable oil

1 lb boneless skinless chicken breasts, cut into ½- to ¾-inch pieces

1 clove garlic, finely chopped

1¾ cups chicken broth (from 32-oz carton)

1 cup uncooked orzo or rosamarina pasta (6 oz)

1 can (14.5 oz) Italian-style stewed tomatoes, undrained

1 medium zucchini, cut lengthwise in half, then crosswise into slices (2 cups)

2 tablespoons shredded Parmesan cheese

1 In 12-inch nonstick skillet, heat oil over medium-high heat. Add chicken and garlic; cook 4 to 6 minutes, stirring frequently, until chicken is browned.

2 Stir in broth and orzo. Heat to boiling. Reduce heat to medium; cover and cook 10 to 15 minutes, stirring occasionally, until orzo is tender and most of liquid is absorbed.

3 Stir in tomatoes and zucchini. Cook uncovered 5 to 10 minutes, stirring occasionally and breaking up tomatoes with spoon, until zucchini is tender and chicken is no longer pink. Sprinkle with cheese.

1 Serving: Calories 350; Total Fat 9g (Saturated Fat 2.5g, Trans Fat 0g); Cholesterol 70mg; Sodium 830mg; Total Carbohydrate 35g (Dietary Fiber 3g); Protein 34g **Exchanges:** 2 Starch, 1 Vegetable, 3½ Very Lean Meat, 1 Fat **Carbohydrate Choices:** 2

Quick Variation For a change of pace and a little stronger cheese flavor, substitute shredded Asiago cheese for the Parmesan. Look for it in containers or packages near the other cheeses.

spring chicken sauté

prep time: 20 Minutes || **start to finish:** 40 Minutes || 4 servings (1½ cups each)

2 cups fresh green beans, cut into 2-inch pieces

1 tablespoon olive oil

1 lb boneless skinless chicken breasts, cut into 1-inch pieces

1 tablespoon chopped fresh oregano or thyme leaves

2 cups sliced yellow summer squash or zucchini

1 can (15 oz) cannellini beans, drained, rinsed

¼ cup reduced-sodium chicken broth

6 cloves garlic, minced

1 cup cherry tomatoes, halved

1 tablespoon chopped fresh basil leaves or Italian (flat-leaf) parsley

¼ teaspoon kosher (coarse) salt

¼ teaspoon pepper

1 In covered 2-quart saucepan, cook green beans in small amount of boiling salted water 8 to 10 minutes or until crisp-tender. Drain; place beans in enough ice water to cover. Let stand until cool. Drain again; set aside.

2 Meanwhile, in 12-inch skillet, heat oil over medium heat. In large bowl, toss chicken with oregano. Add chicken to skillet; cook 5 to 6 minutes, stirring frequently, until no longer pink in center. Remove chicken from skillet; set aside.

3 Add squash to same skillet; cook and stir over medium-high heat 3 minutes. Stir in green beans, cannellini beans, broth, garlic and chicken. Heat to boiling. Add tomatoes, basil, salt and pepper; cook about 1 minute longer or until thoroughly heated.

1 Serving: Calories 250; Total Fat 5g (Saturated Fat 1g, Trans Fat 0g); Cholesterol 65mg; Sodium 410mg; Total Carbohydrate 24g (Dietary Fiber 8g); Protein 35g **Exchanges:** 1½ Starch, 1 Vegetable, 4 Very Lean Meat **Carbohydrate Choices:** 1½

parmesan chicken with fettucine

prep time: **20 Minutes** || start to finish: **25 Minutes** || **4 servings**

1 tablespoon vegetable oil

2 cloves garlic, finely chopped

2 cups marinara sauce

2 cups water

1 package (9 oz) refrigerated fettuccine

1 bag (12 oz) frozen cut green beans, thawed

2 cups cubed cooked chicken

½ cup grated Parmesan cheese

1 In 12-inch skillet, heat oil over medium heat. Add garlic; cook about 30 seconds, stirring occasionally, until softened. Stir in marinara sauce and water. Cover; heat to boiling over medium heat.

2 Add fettuccine and green beans; stir to separate fettuccine. Return to boiling. Cover; boil 3 to 5 minutes or until beans are tender.

3 Remove from heat. Sprinkle with cheese. Cover; let stand 2 minutes or until cheese is melted.

1 Serving: Calories 590; Total Fat 18g (Saturated Fat 4.5g, Trans Fat 0g); Cholesterol 115mg; Sodium 1090mg; Total Carbohydrate 71g (Dietary Fiber 6g); Protein 36g **Exchanges:** 3½ Starch, 2½ Vegetable, 3 Very Lean Meat, 2½ Fat **Carbohydrate Choices:** 5

time-saver To quickly thaw the green beans, place them in a colander or strainer, then rinse with cool water until thawed. Drain well.

parmesan chicken ziti with artichokes and spinach

prep time: **35 Minutes** || start to finish: **35 Minutes** || **6 servings (2 cups each)**

4   cups water

2   cans (12 oz each) evaporated milk

1   teaspoon salt

2   cloves garlic, finely chopped

1   lb uncooked ziti pasta

2   teaspoons cornstarch

2   cups shredded deli rotisserie chicken

1   can (14 oz) artichoke hearts, drained, coarsely chopped

2½ cups shredded Parmesan cheese (10 oz)

    Juice of 2 medium lemons (about ⅔ cup)

2   tablespoons butter

4   cups baby spinach leaves (5-oz package)

½   teaspoon pepper, if desired

1 In Dutch oven or large saucepot, heat water, 1 can of the evaporated milk, the salt, garlic and pasta to simmering over medium heat. Simmer 12 to 14 minutes, stirring frequently, until pasta is tender.

2 In medium bowl, beat remaining can of evaporated milk and the cornstarch; stir in chicken and artichoke hearts. Add to mixture in Dutch oven; return to simmering, and continue to simmer 1 to 3 minutes or until thickened and mixture coats back of spoon.

3 Remove from heat; stir in half of the cheese and the lemon juice. Stir until cheese melts, then add remaining cheese (reserving ¼ cup for serving, if desired) and butter; stir again.

4 Add spinach, and stir until wilted. Sprinkle with pepper and serve with reserved cheese.

1 Serving: Calories 800; Total Fat 27g (Saturated Fat 14g, Trans Fat 1g); Cholesterol 100mg; Sodium 1650mg; Total Carbohydrate 87g (Dietary Fiber 8g); Protein 52g **Exchanges:** 4½ Starch, 1 Low-Fat Milk, 1 Vegetable, 4 Lean Meat, 1½ Fat **Carbohydrate Choices:** 6

Quick Variation Baby kale or chard makes a great stand-in for spinach in this recipe.

quick creamy parmesan chicken penne

prep time: 15 Minutes || **start to finish:** 30 Minutes || **4 servings**

- 1 **pouch (9 oz) creamy Parmesan-basil cooking sauce**
- 1 **tablespoon butter**
- 1½ **cups water**
  Salt and pepper
- 2 **cups uncooked penne pasta**
- 2 **cups chopped cooked chicken**
- ⅓ **cup shredded Parmesan cheese**
- 1 **cup diced tomato**
- ¼ **cups Italian-style panko crispy bread crumbs**

1 In 10-inch skillet, heat cooking sauce, butter, water, and salt and pepper (as desired) to boiling.

2 Stir in pasta; reduce heat to medium. Cover; cook about 10 minutes, stirring occasionally, until pasta is tender. Stir in chicken and cheese.

3 Top with tomato and bread crumbs. Serve immediately.

1 Serving: Calories 670; Total Fat 17g (Saturated Fat 5g, Trans Fat 0g); Cholesterol 70mg; Sodium 1810mg; Total Carbohydrate 84g (Dietary Fiber 10g); Protein 44g **Exchanges:** 4½ Starch, ½ Skim Milk, 1½ Vegetable, 2 Very Lean Meat, 1 Lean Meat, ½ Medium-Fat Meat, 1½ Fat **Carbohydrate Choices:** 5½

turkey stroganoff skillet supper

prep time: 25 Minutes ‖ **start to finish:** 35 Minutes ‖ **4 servings (1⅓ cups each)**

¾ cup chicken broth (from 32-oz carton)

1 jar (12 oz) turkey gravy

2½ cups uncooked wide egg noodles (4 oz)

1 cup sliced fresh carrots (2 medium)

1 cup frozen sweet peas (from 12-oz bag)

½ cup sour cream

⅛ teaspoon ground nutmeg

⅛ teaspoon pepper

2 cups cubed cooked turkey

1 In 10-inch skillet, mix broth and gravy until well blended. Heat to boiling. Stir in noodles, carrots, peas, sour cream, nutmeg and pepper. Return to boiling. Reduce heat to low; cover and simmer 10 minutes.

2 Stir in turkey. Cook 3 to 4 minutes, stirring occasionally, until noodles and vegetables are tender.

1 Serving: Calories 400; Total Fat 17g (Saturated Fat 6g, Trans Fat 0g); Cholesterol 105mg; Sodium 1020mg; Total Carbohydrate 32g (Dietary Fiber 3g); Protein 29g **Exchanges:** 1½ Starch, ½ Other Carbohydrate, 1 Vegetable, 3 Lean Meat, 1½ Fat **Carbohydrate Choices:** 2

curried turkey stir-fry

prep time: 30 Minutes || **start to finish:** 30 Minutes || 4 servings (1¼ cups each)

1¾ cups uncooked instant brown rice

2 cups water

¼ teaspoon salt

2 teaspoons vegetable oil

1 lb turkey breast strips for stir-fry

1 medium red bell pepper, cut into thin strips

2 cups small fresh broccoli florets

1¼ cups reduced-sodium chicken broth (from 32-oz carton)

4 teaspoons cornstarch

4 teaspoons curry powder

½ teaspoon ground ginger

¼ teaspoon salt

1 Cook rice as directed on package, using water and ¼ teaspoon salt.

2 Meanwhile, in 12-inch nonstick skillet, heat oil over medium-high heat. Add turkey; cook 5 to 8 minutes, stirring frequently, until browned. Stir in bell pepper and broccoli. Cook 2 minutes.

3 In small bowl, mix remaining ingredients. Stir into turkey and vegetables. Heat to boiling. Reduce heat; cover and cook 2 to 3 minutes or until vegetables are crisp-tender and turkey is no longer pink in center. Serve over rice.

1 Serving: Calories 470; Total Fat 7g (Saturated Fat 1.5g, Trans Fat 0g); Cholesterol 75mg; Sodium 530mg; Total Carbohydrate 71g (Dietary Fiber 8g); Protein 37g **Exchanges:** 4½ Starch, 1 Vegetable, 3 Very Lean Meat **Carbohydrate Choices:** 4

Quick Variation If you can't find the ready-to-cook turkey breast strips, you can purchase turkey breast tenderloins and cut them into strips.

asparagus and turkey sausage skillet

prep time: 15 Minutes ‖ start to finish: 25 Minutes ‖ 4 servings

1 tablespoon olive or vegetable oil

1 package (19.5 oz) lean Italian turkey sausages, casings removed, cut into ½-inch slices

1 large onion, coarsely chopped (1 cup)

1 cup chicken broth (from 32-oz carton)

1 cup water

1 cup uncooked orzo or rosamarina pasta (6 oz)

1 lb fresh asparagus spears, trimmed, cut into 1-inch pieces

2 tablespoons sliced pimientos (from 4-oz jar)

1 In 12-inch nonstick skillet, heat oil over medium-high heat. Add sausage and onion; cook 2 minutes, stirring occasionally.

2 Stir in broth and water. Heat to boiling. Stir in orzo; boil 2 minutes.

3 Add asparagus and pimientos. Reduce heat to medium; cover and return to boiling. Cook 8 to 10 minutes or until orzo is tender.

1 Serving: Calories 470; Total Fat 19g (Saturated Fat 4g, Trans Fat 0.5g); Cholesterol 125mg; Sodium 1140mg; Total Carbohydrate 34g (Dietary Fiber 3g); Protein 40g **Exchanges:** 2 Starch, 1½ Vegetable, 1½ Very Lean Meat, 2 Lean Meat, 2½ Fat **Carbohydrate Choices:** 2

Quick Variation Frozen asparagus is a great substitute for the fresh. One 9- or 10-ounce box (about 1½ cups) is the right amount.

cheesy steak and potato skillet

prep time: 30 Minutes || start to finish: 30 Minutes || 4 servings

1 lb boneless beef sirloin steak, cut into 4 serving pieces

¾ teaspoon seasoned salt

½ teaspoon garlic-pepper blend

2 tablespoons butter

1½ cups frozen bell pepper and onion stir-fry (from 1-lb bag)

1 bag (20 oz) refrigerated home-style potato slices

1 cup shredded American-Cheddar cheese blend (4 oz)

1 Sprinkle beef pieces with ¼ teaspoon of the seasoned salt and ¼ teaspoon of the garlic-pepper blend. In 12-inch nonstick skillet, cook beef over medium-high heat 3 to 4 minutes, turning once or twice, until browned and desired doneness. Remove from skillet; cover to keep warm.

2 In same skillet, melt butter over medium heat. Add stir-fry vegetables; cook 2 minutes, stirring frequently. Add potatoes; sprinkle with remaining ½ teaspoon seasoned salt and ¼ teaspoon garlic-pepper blend. Cook uncovered 8 to 10 minutes, stirring frequently, until tender.

3 Place beef in skillet with potatoes, pushing potatoes around beef. Cook 1 to 2 minutes, turning beef once, until hot. Sprinkle with cheese. Cover; heat until cheese is melted.

1 Serving: Calories 470; Total Fat 19g (Saturated Fat 11g, Trans Fat 0.5g); Cholesterol 120mg; Sodium 700mg; Total Carbohydrate 33g (Dietary Fiber 2g); Protein 40g **Exchanges:** 2 Starch, 1 Vegetable, 4½ Lean Meat, 1 Fat **Carbohydrate Choices:** 2

healthy twist This easy skillet dish has everything going for it—it's high in calcium and iron and low in carbohydrates.

beefy rice skillet

prep time: **25 Minutes** || start to finish: **30 Minutes** || **4 servings**

1 lb lean (at least 80%) ground beef

2½ cups hot water

¾ cup ready-to-eat baby-cut carrots, cut lengthwise in half

1 tablespoon butter

¼ teaspoon pepper

1 package (6.4 oz) four-cheese rice and pasta blend

1½ cups fresh broccoli florets

½ cup cherry or grape tomatoes, cut in half

1 In 12-inch skillet, cook beef over medium-high heat 5 to 7 minutes, stirring occasionally, until thoroughly cooked; drain.

2 Stir water, carrots, butter, pepper, rice mixture and contents of seasoning packet into beef. Heat to boiling. Reduce heat; cover and cook about 15 minutes or until rice and carrots are almost tender, stirring occasionally.

3 Stir in broccoli. Cover; cook 5 minutes or until crisp-tender. Stir in tomatoes. Cook uncovered about 1 minute or just until heated.

1 Serving: Calories 420; Total Fat 20g (Saturated Fat 9g, Trans Fat 1g); Cholesterol 80mg; Sodium 700mg; Total Carbohydrate 35g (Dietary Fiber 2g); Protein 25g **Exchanges:** 2 Starch, 1 Vegetable, 2 Lean Meat, ½ Medium-Fat Meat, 2 Fat **Carbohydrate Choices:** 2

time-saver Make this recipe even easier by simply purchasing already-cut veggies in the produce section or at the salad bar in the grocery store.

pasta with italian meatballs

prep time: **30 Minutes** || start to finish: **30 Minutes** || **4 servings**

1 cup water

1 jar (25.5 oz) tomato pasta sauce (any flavor)

1½ cups uncooked elbow macaroni

20 frozen cooked Italian-style or regular meatballs (1 inch)

1 can (2¼ oz) sliced ripe olives, drained

Grated Parmesan cheese, if desired

1 In 10-inch skillet, heat water and pasta sauce to boiling. Stir in macaroni, meatballs and olives. Return to boiling.

2 Reduce heat to medium. Cover; cook 15 to 20 minutes, stirring occasionally, until macaroni is tender. Sprinkle with cheese.

1 Serving: Calories 790; Total Fat 32g (Saturated Fat 10g, Trans Fat 0); Cholesterol 145mg; Sodium 1940mg; Total Carbohydrate 92g (Dietary Fiber 6g); Protein 39g **Exchanges:** 5½ Starch, 2 Vegetable, 3 High-Fat Meat **Carbohydrate Choices:**

spaghetti ragu with fresh basil

prep time: **25 Minutes** || start to finish: **35 Minutes** || **6 servings (1⅔ cups each)**

- 2 tablespoons olive oil
- 2 medium onions, diced (about 3 cups)
- 2 medium carrots, diced (about 1 cup)
- 1 teaspoon salt
- 1 lb lean (at least 80%) ground beef
- ¼ cup canned tomato paste
- 1 can (28 oz) fire-roasted diced tomatoes, undrained
- 1 carton (32 oz) beef broth
- 2 teaspoons dried Italian seasoning
- ½ teaspoon crushed red pepper flakes
- 1 lb uncooked spaghetti
- ½ cup shredded Parmesan cheese (2 oz)
- ¼ cup thinly sliced fresh basil leaves

1 In Dutch oven or large saucepan, heat oil over medium-high heat until hot. Cook onions, carrots and salt in oil 5 to 8 minutes or until softened. Add beef; cook 5 to 8 minutes, stirring frequently, until browned.

2 Stir in tomato paste and tomatoes. Stir in broth, Italian seasoning, and red pepper; heat to simmering. Break spaghetti in half, then thoroughly rinse under cold water. Tuck spaghetti into simmering liquid, covering completely. Reduce heat to medium-low; cook 13 to 15 minutes or until spaghetti is tender and sauce is reduced slightly.

3 Top with Parmesan cheese and basil.

1 Serving: Calories 630; Total Fat 18g (Saturated Fat 6g, Trans Fat 0.5g); Cholesterol 55mg; Sodium 1520mg; Total Carbohydrate 86g (Dietary Fiber 7g); Protein 32g **Exchanges:** 2 Starch, 3 Other Carbohydrate, 2 Vegetable, 3 Lean Meat, 2 Fat **Carbohydrate Choices:** 6

Quick Variation Mix up this dish with different shapes of pasta, like penne or fusilli.

healthy twist For an extra veggie boost, stir in a couple of cups of spinach or baby kale just before serving.

beef and kasha mexicana

prep time: 25 Minutes ‖ **start to finish:** 25 Minutes ‖ 6 servings (1⅓ cups each)

1 lb extra-lean (at least 90%) ground beef

1 medium onion, chopped (½ cup)

1 cup uncooked buckwheat kernels or groats (kasha)

1 can (14½ oz) diced tomatoes, undrained

1 can (4½ oz) chopped green chiles, undrained

2 cups frozen whole kernel corn, thawed

1 package (1 oz) 40% less-sodium taco seasoning mix

1½ cups water

1 cup shredded reduced-fat Cheddar cheese (4 oz)

2 tablespoons chopped fresh cilantro, if desired

2 tablespoons sliced ripe olives, if desired

1 In 12-inch skillet, cook ground beef and onion over medium-high heat 5 to 7 minutes, stirring occasionally, until beef is thoroughly cooked; drain. Stir in kasha until kernels are moistened by beef mixture.

2 Stir in tomatoes, chiles, corn, taco seasoning mix and water. Heat to boiling. Reduce heat to low; cover and simmer 5 to 7 minutes, stirring occasionally, until kasha is tender.

3 Sprinkle cheese over kasha mixture. Cover; cook 2 to 3 minutes or until cheese is melted. Sprinkle with cilantro and olives.

1 Serving: Calories 300; Total Fat 9g (Saturated Fat 3.5g, Trans Fat 0g); Cholesterol 50mg; Sodium 990mg; Total Carbohydrate 33g (Dietary Fiber 5g); Protein 23g **Exchanges:** 2 Starch, 2½ Lean Meat **Carbohydrate Choices:** 2

beef and salsa with dumplings

prep time: **15 Minutes** || start to finish: **40 Minutes** || **6 servings**

1 lb lean (at least 80%) ground beef

1 jar (16 oz) chunky-style salsa (2 cups)

1 can (15 oz) dark red kidney beans, undrained

1 can (7 oz) vacuum-packed whole kernel corn, undrained

1 can (8 oz) tomato sauce

2 teaspoons chili powder

1½ cups Original Bisquick mix

½ cup milk

½ cup shredded Colby–Monterey Jack cheese (2 oz), if desired

1 In 12-inch skillet, cook beef over medium heat, stirring occasionally, until browned; drain. Stir in salsa, beans, corn, tomato sauce and 1 teaspoon of the chili powder. Heat to boiling; reduce heat to low.

2 In medium bowl, stir Bisquick mix, remaining 1 teaspoon chili powder and the milk until soft dough forms. Drop dough by 6 spoonfuls onto simmering beef mixture.

3 Cover; cook about 20 minutes or until dumplings are light and fluffy inside. Sprinkle with cheese. Cover; cook about 2 minutes or until cheese is melted.

1 Serving: Calories 390; Total Fat 13g (Saturated Fat 4.5g, Trans Fat 1.5g); Cholesterol 50mg; Sodium 1510mg; Total Carbohydrate 46g (Dietary Fiber 5g); Protein 21g **Exchanges:** 3 Starch, 2 Lean Meat, 1 Fat **Carbohydrate Choices:** 3

Quick Variation Make an equally delicious and quick meal by substituting ground turkey breast for the ground beef.

healthy twist To reduce the fat to about 7 grams and the calories to about 340 per serving, use 12 ounces extra-lean (at least 90%) ground beef and 1½ cups Bisquick Heart Smart mix.

meaty italian ramen skillet

prep time: **30 Minutes** || start to finish: **35 Minutes** || **4 servings**

2 packages (3 oz each) beef-flavor ramen noodle soup mix

1 lb lean (at least 80%) ground beef

24 slices pepperoni (1 to 1¼ inches in diameter)

1 can (14.5 oz) diced tomatoes with basil, garlic and oregano, undrained

1 cup water

1 small green bell pepper, cut into ½-inch pieces (½ cup)

1 cup shredded mozzarella cheese (4 oz)

1 Break blocks of noodles in half (reserve 1 seasoning packet; discard second packet). Set aside.

2 In 10-inch skillet, cook beef and pepperoni over medium-high heat 5 to 7 minutes, stirring occasionally, until beef is thoroughly cooked; drain.

3 Stir in tomatoes, water and reserved seasoning packet. Heat to boiling. Stir in noodles and bell pepper. Cook 3 to 5 minutes, stirring occasionally, until noodles are tender. Remove skillet from heat.

4 Sprinkle cheese around edge of noodle mixture. Cover; let stand about 5 minutes or until cheese is melted.

1 Serving: Calories 570; Total Fat 34g (Saturated Fat 14g, Trans Fat 2g); Cholesterol 120mg; Sodium 960mg; Total Carbohydrate 27g (Dietary Fiber 2g); Protein 39g **Exchanges:** 2 Starch, 1 Vegetable, 3½ Medium-Fat Meat, 2 Fat **Carbohydrate Choices:** 2

healthy twist Sodium is reduced in this recipe because it only calls for one of the ramen seasoning packets.

parmesan orzo and meatballs

prep time: 30 Minutes || start to finish: 30 Minutes || 4 servings

1½ cups frozen bell pepper and onion stir-fry (from 1-lb bag)

2 tablespoons Italian dressing

1¾ cups beef broth (from 32-oz carton)

1 cup uncooked orzo or rosamarina pasta (6 oz)

16 frozen cooked Italian-style meatballs (from 16-oz bag)

1 large tomato, chopped (1 cup)

2 tablespoons chopped fresh parsley

¼ cup shredded Parmesan cheese (1 oz)

1 In 12-inch nonstick skillet, cook stir-fry vegetables and dressing over medium-high heat 2 minutes. Stir in broth; heat to boiling. Stir in pasta and meatballs. Return to boiling. Reduce heat to low; cover and cook 10 minutes, stirring occasionally.

2 Stir in tomato. Cover; cook 3 to 5 minutes longer or until most of liquid has been absorbed and pasta is tender. Stir in parsley. Sprinkle with cheese.

1 Serving: Calories 500; Total Fat 21g (Saturated Fat 7g, Trans Fat 1g); Cholesterol 125mg; Sodium 1240mg; Total Carbohydrate 45g (Dietary Fiber 4g); Protein 32g **Exchanges:** 2 Starch, ½ Other Carbohydrate, 1 Vegetable, 3½ Medium-Fat Meat, ½ Fat **Carbohydrate Choices:** 3

balsamic pork chops with quinoa

prep time: **20 Minutes** || start to finish: **40 Minutes** || **4 servings**

5 teaspoons vegetable oil

1 medium onion, cut into wedges

4 boneless pork loin chops, ½ to ¾ inch thick (6 oz each), trimmed of fat

¾ teaspoon seasoned salt

¼ teaspoon dried thyme leaves

¼ teaspoon pepper

¾ cup water

¼ cup white balsamic vinegar

½ cup uncooked quinoa

2 tablespoons chopped fresh parsley

2 cups bite-size fresh broccoli florets

1½ cups frozen peach slices (from 16-oz bag)

1 In 12-inch nonstick skillet, heat 2 teaspoons of the oil over medium-high heat. Add onion; cook 5 minutes, stirring occasionally, until onion begins to brown. Remove from skillet; set aside.

2 Season both sides of pork chops with ¼ teaspoon of the seasoned salt, the thyme and pepper. Heat remaining 3 teaspoons oil in same skillet over medium heat. Add pork; cook 2 to 3 minutes on each side or until browned. Transfer from skillet to plate.

3 Add water, vinegar, quinoa, parsley, cooked onion and remaining ½ teaspoon seasoned salt to skillet. Heat to boiling. Reduce heat; place pork and any juices on top of quinoa mixture. Cover; simmer 10 minutes.

4 Add broccoli and peaches; cover and cook about 10 minutes longer or until quinoa is tender and meat thermometer inserted in center of pork reads 145°F.

1 Serving: Calories 470; Total Fat 21g (Saturated Fat 6g, Trans Fat 0g); Cholesterol 115mg; Sodium 350mg; Total Carbohydrate 27g (Dietary Fiber 4g); Protein 44g **Exchanges:** 1 Starch, ½ Fruit, 1 Vegetable, 5½ Lean Meat, 1 Fat **Carbohydrate Choices:** 2

creamy mushroom pork chops

prep time: 30 Minutes || **start to finish:** 30 Minutes || 4 servings

4   slices bacon, cut into
    1-inch pieces

4   boneless pork loin chops,
    about ½ inch thick
    (1¼ lb), trimmed of fat

½   teaspoon garlic salt

⅛   teaspoon pepper

1   can (18 oz) ready-to-
    serve creamy mushroom
    soup

¼   cup sliced green onions
    (4 medium)

½   cup sour cream

    Chopped fresh parsley or
    other herbs, if desired

1 In 12-inch nonstick skillet, cook bacon over medium heat, stirring occasionally, until crisp. Remove bacon with slotted spoon; drain on paper towels. Drain all but 1 tablespoon bacon drippings from skillet.

2 Sprinkle pork chops with garlic salt and pepper. Add pork chops to bacon drippings in skillet. Cook over medium heat 3 to 4 minutes, turning once, until lightly browned. Remove pork from skillet; set aside. Stir in soup and green onions; heat to boiling, stirring occasionally. Reduce heat; simmer uncovered 5 minutes, stirring occasionally.

3 Return pork to skillet. Cover; simmer 8 to 10 minutes, turning once, until pork is no longer pink and meat thermometer inserted in center reads 145°F. Remove from heat. Stir in sour cream; sprinkle with bacon and parsley.

1 Serving: Calories 390; Total Fat 25g (Saturated Fat 9g, Trans Fat 0g); Cholesterol 110mg; Sodium 800mg; Total Carbohydrate 7g (Dietary Fiber 0g); Protein 35g **Exchanges:** ½ Other Carbohydrate, 4½ Very Lean Meat, ½ High-Fat Meat, 3½ Fat **Carbohydrate Choices:** ½

pizza quinoa with sausage, onion and pepper

prep time: 30 Minutes || **start to finish:** 1 Hour || 8 servings (1½ cups each)

1 lb bulk spicy Italian pork sausage

2 tablespoons olive oil

1 red onion, thinly sliced (about 2 cups)

1 green bell pepper, cut into thin strips (about 1 cup)

8 oz sliced fresh mushrooms

1½ teaspoons salt

1 teaspoon dried Italian seasoning

1 package (12 oz) uncooked quinoa, rinsed (2 cups)

4 cups milk

2 cups shredded mozzarella cheese (8 oz)

2 cups cherry tomatoes (10½ oz), quartered

½ cup thinly sliced fresh basil leaves

Shredded Parmesan cheese, if desired

1 In 5-quart nonstick Dutch oven or stockpot, cook sausage over medium heat until no longer pink. Drain; transfer to large bowl. Cover with foil; set aside.

2 Wipe out Dutch oven with paper towel. Add 1 tablespoon of the oil; heat over medium heat until hot. Add onion and bell pepper; cook 3 to 5 minutes or until tender. Using slotted spoon, transfer onion and bell pepper to bowl with sausage; replace foil, and set aside.

3 Increase heat to high. Add remaining 1 tablespoon oil, the mushrooms, salt and Italian seasoning. Cook 5 to 7 minutes or until mushrooms brown and liquid evaporates. Transfer to bowl of sausage and vegetables; cover with foil to keep warm.

4 Wipe out Dutch oven. Add quinoa; cook over medium heat 1 to 2 minutes, stirring occasionally, until fragrant. Slowly stir in milk. Heat to simmering over high heat, stirring occasionally. Cover; reduce heat to low. Cook 20 to 25 minutes or until liquid is absorbed and quinoa is thoroughly cooked. Stir in sausage and vegetables.

5 Remove from heat; stir in mozzarella cheese. Top with tomatoes, basil and Parmesan cheese.

1 Serving: Calories 450; Total Fat 22g (Saturated Fat 8g, Trans Fat 0g); Cholesterol 45mg; Sodium 890mg; Total Carbohydrate 39g (Dietary Fiber 4g); Protein 24g **Exchanges:** 2 Starch, 1 Vegetable, 1 Medium-Fat Meat, 1½ High-Fat Meat, 1 Fat **Carbohydrate Choices:** 2½

beer-cheese kielbasa with tortellini

prep time: **30 Minutes** || start to finish: **30 Minutes** || **4 servings (1½ cups each)**

1 package (9 oz) refrigerated three-cheese tortellini

¾ cup water

⅓ cup all-purpose flour

1 cup light beer

⅓ cup sliced green onions with tops

3 tablespoons chili sauce

2 teaspoons ground mustard

½ teaspoon salt

1 package (14 oz) cooked kielbasa or other smoked sausage, cut diagonally into 1-inch-thick slices

1½ cups shredded Cheddar cheese (6 oz)

2 tablespoons diced roasted red bell peppers (from a jar)

1 Fill 12-inch nonstick skillet half full with water (about 6 cups). Heat to boiling. Add tortellini; cook uncovered minimum time as directed on bag, stirring occasionally. Drain.

2 In 1-cup measuring cup, stir ¾ cup water and the flour with whisk until smooth; pour into same skillet. Stir in beer, green onions, chili sauce, mustard and salt. Heat to boiling. Reduce heat; simmer uncovered 1 minute, stirring constantly, until thickened.

3 Gently fold in tortellini and kielbasa. Cover; cook over medium-low heat about 5 minutes or until kielbasa is hot.

4 Fold in cheese, ½ cup at a time, until melted. Remove from heat; top with roasted peppers.

1 Serving: Calories 740; Total Fat 46g (Saturated Fat 21g, Trans Fat 1g); Cholesterol 125mg; Sodium 1950mg; Total Carbohydrate 46g (Dietary Fiber 3g); Protein 32g **Exchanges:** 2 Starch, 1 Other Carbohydrate, 4 High-Fat Meat, 2½ Fat **Carbohydrate Choices:** 3

Quick Variation Add 1 cup frozen sweet peas with the kielbasa.

no-bake cheesy skillet lasagna

prep time: 25 Minutes | start to finish: 30 Minutes | 6 servings

1 lb bulk Italian pork sausage

2 cups water

1 bag (16-oz) frozen red bell pepper and onion stir-fry, thawed, drained

1 can (18 oz) creamy three-cheese cooking sauce

3 cups uncooked mini lasagna (mafalda) noodles or medium egg noodles (6 oz)

1 teaspoon dried Italian seasoning

1 cup shredded mozzarella cheese (4 oz)

Chopped or whole fresh basil leaves, if desired

1 In 12-inch skillet, cook sausage over medium-high heat 5 to 7 minutes, stirring occasionally, until no longer pink; drain.

2 Stir in all remaining ingredients except cheese and basil. Heat to boiling, stirring occasionally.

3 Reduce heat to medium; simmer uncovered about 10 minutes, stirring occasionally, until pasta is tender. Remove from heat; sprinkle with cheese. Cover; let stand 2 to 3 minutes or until cheese is melted. Sprinkle with basil.

1 Serving: Calories 450; Total Fat 24g (Saturated Fat 9g, Trans Fat 0g); Cholesterol 50mg; Sodium 1060mg; Total Carbohydrate 35g (Dietary Fiber 2g); Protein 23g **Exchanges:** 2 Starch, 1½ Vegetable, ½ Medium-Fat Meat, 1½ High-Fat Meat, 1½ Fat **Carbohydrate Choices:** 2

weeknight paella

prep time: **15 Minutes** || start to finish: **30 Minutes** || **6 servings (1½ cups each)**

2 tablespoons olive or vegetable oil

1 package (5.9 oz) chicken-garlic rice and vermicelli mix

1 cup frozen bell pepper and onion stir-fry (from 1-lb bag)

1¾ cups chicken broth (from 32-oz carton)

¾ cup water

1 dried bay leaf

8 oz fully cooked chorizo sausage, cut into bite-size pieces

½ cup frozen baby sweet peas

1 deli rotisserie chicken (2 lb), cut into 6 serving pieces

1 cup cooked deveined peeled medium shrimp, thawed if frozen, tail shells removed

1 In 12-inch skillet, heat oil over medium-high heat. Add rice mix and stir-fry vegetables; cook 2 to 3 minutes, stirring constantly, until rice mix begins to brown.

2 Stir in broth, water, bay leaf and seasoning packet from rice mix. Heat to boiling. Reduce heat to low; cover and simmer 5 minutes.

3 Stir in sausage and peas. Add chicken. Heat to boiling over medium-high heat. Reduce heat to low; cover and simmer 10 minutes.

4 Stir in shrimp. Cover; cook about 5 minutes or until shrimp and chicken are thoroughly heated. Remove bay leaf before serving.

1 Serving: Calories 440; Total Fat 26g (Saturated Fat 8g, Trans Fat 0g); Cholesterol 155mg; Sodium 1330mg; Total Carbohydrate 12g (Dietary Fiber 0g); Protein 41g **Exchanges:** ½ Starch, 1 Vegetable, 5½ Lean Meat, 2 Fat **Carbohydrate Choices:** 1

time-saver Chorizo is a spicy Spanish or Mexican pork sausage sold fully cooked or fresh. Using the cooked Spanish variety is definitely a time-saver, but you can use fresh Mexican chorizo instead. Just be sure to cook it thoroughly before adding to the recipe.

huevos rancheros

prep time: 45 Minutes || start to finish: 45 Minutes || 6 servings

8 oz bulk uncooked chorizo or pork sausage

Vegetable oil

6 corn tortillas (6- to 7-inch)

1¼ cups chunky-style salsa

6 fried eggs

1½ cups shredded Cheddar cheese (6 oz)

1 In 8-inch skillet, cook sausage over medium heat 8 to 10 minutes, stirring occasionally, until no longer pink; drain. Remove sausage from skillet; keep warm.

2 In same skillet, heat ⅛ inch oil over medium heat just until hot. Cook 1 tortilla at a time in oil about 1 minute, turning once, until crisp; drain.

3 In 1-quart saucepan, heat salsa, stirring occasionally, until hot.

4 Spread 1 tablespoon salsa over each tortilla to soften. Place 1 fried egg on each tortilla. Top with salsa, sausage, additional salsa and cheese.

1 Serving: Calories 460; Total Fat 33g (Saturated Fat 14g, Trans Fat 1g); Cholesterol 275mg; Sodium 1100mg; Total Carbohydrate 16g (Dietary Fiber 2g); Protein 25g **Exchanges:** 1 Starch, 3 High-Fat Meat, 2 Fat **Carbohydrate Choices:** 1

savory italian frittata

prep time: **20 Minutes** || start to finish: **30 Minutes** || **6 servings**

8 eggs

1 tablespoon chopped fresh or ½ teaspoon dried basil leaves

1 tablespoon chopped fresh or ½ teaspoon dried mint leaves

1 tablespoon chopped fresh or ½ teaspoon dried sage leaves

1 tablespoon grated Parmesan cheese

½ teaspoon salt

⅛ teaspoon pepper

¼ cup diced prosciutto or cooked ham (2 oz)

1 tablespoon butter

1 small onion, finely chopped (⅓ cup)

1 In medium bowl, beat all ingredients except prosciutto, butter and onion thoroughly with fork or whisk until well mixed. Stir in prosciutto.

2 In 10-inch nonstick skillet, melt butter over medium-high heat. Add onion; cook 4 to 5 minutes, stirring frequently, until crisp-tender.

3 Reduce heat to medium-low. Pour egg mixture into skillet. Cover; cook 9 to 11 minutes or until eggs are set around edge and lightly browned on bottom. Cut into wedges to serve.

1 Serving: Calories 140; Total Fat 10g (Saturated Fat 3.5g, Trans Fat 0g); Cholesterol 295mg; Sodium 450mg; Total Carbohydrate 1g (Dietary Fiber 0g); Protein 11g
Exchanges: 1½ Medium-Fat Meat, ½ Fat **Carbohydrate Choices:** 0

healthy twist To reduce the fat to about 3 grams and calories to about 80 per serving, substitute 2 cups fat-free egg product for the eggs. Substitute cooked turkey ham for the prosciutto.

smoked salmon and herb frittata

prep time: **30 Minutes** ‖ start to finish: **30 Minutes** ‖ **4 servings**

6 **eggs**

2 **tablespoons half-and-half or milk**

2 **tablespoons chopped fresh chives (½-inch pieces)**

1 **tablespoon coarsely chopped fresh dill weed**

¼ **teaspoon pepper**

1 **package (3 oz) sliced smoked salmon, cut into 1½-inch pieces**

2 **teaspoons olive oil**

3 **oz cream cheese (from 8-oz package), softened**

Lemon wedges

1 In medium bowl, beat eggs, half-and-half, chives, dill and pepper. Gently fold in salmon.

2 In 9- or 10-inch nonstick skillet with sloping sides, heat oil over low heat. Pour egg mixture into skillet. Using 2 teaspoons, drop cream cheese in pieces over egg mixture.

3 Cover; cook 12 to 15 minutes or until lightly browned and bottom is set, lifting edges occasionally to allow uncooked egg mixture to flow to bottom of skillet. Cut into wedges. Garnish with lemon wedges.

1 Serving: Calories 240; Total Fat 19g (Saturated Fat 8g, Trans Fat 0g); Cholesterol 350mg; Sodium 330mg; Total Carbohydrate 2g (Dietary Fiber 0g); Protein 15g **Exchanges:** ½ Lean Meat, 1½ Medium-Fat Meat, 2 Fat **Carbohydrate Choices:** 0

Heirloom Recipe and New Twist

CLASSIC

ramen shrimp and veggies

prep time: **20 Minutes** || start to finish: **20 Minutes** || **4 servings**

- 2 **teaspoons vegetable oil**
- 1 **lb uncooked deveined peeled medium shrimp, thawed if frozen, tail shells removed**
- 2 **cups water**
- 1 **package (3 oz) Oriental-flavor ramen noodle soup mix**
- 1 **package (16 oz) fresh stir-fry vegetables (4 cups)**
- ¼ **cup stir-fry sauce**

1 In 12-inch nonstick skillet, heat oil over medium-high heat. Add shrimp; cook 2 to 4 minutes, stirring occasionally, until pink. Remove shrimp from skillet; keep warm.

2 In same skillet, heat water to boiling. Break up noodles from soup mix into water; stir until slightly softened. Stir in vegetables. Heat to boiling. Boil 4 to 6 minutes, stirring occasionally, until vegetables are crisp-tender.

3 Stir in seasoning packet from soup mix and stir-fry sauce. Cook 3 to 5 minutes, stirring frequently, until hot. Stir in shrimp.

1 Serving: Calories 210; Total Fat 4.5g (Saturated Fat 1g, Trans Fat 1g); Cholesterol 160mg; Sodium 1160mg; Total Carbohydrate 21g (Dietary Fiber 3g); Protein 22g **Exchanges:** 1 Starch, 1 Vegetable, 2½ Very Lean Meat, ½ Fat **Carbohydrate Choices:** 1½

Quick Variation Substitute 1 pound beef strips for stir-fry (from the meat case) for the shrimp. In step 1, cook beef 3 to 5 minutes, stirring occasionally, until no longer pink.

thai ramen shrimp and veggies

prep time: 20 Minutes ‖ **start to finish:** 20 Minutes ‖ 4 servings

- 2 teaspoons vegetable oil
- 1 lb uncooked deveined peeled medium shrimp, thawed if frozen, tail shells removed
- 1 can (14 oz) coconut milk (not cream of coconut)
- 2 tablespoons water
- 1 package (3 oz) Oriental-flavor ramen noodle soup mix
- 1 package (16 oz) fresh stir-fry vegetables (4 cups)
- ¼ cup Thai peanut sauce
- 1 tablespoon chopped fresh cilantro
- 1 teaspoon finely grated lime peel
- Crushed red pepper flakes, if desired
- ¼ cup salted peanuts or cashews

1 In 12-inch nonstick skillet, heat oil over medium-high heat. Add shrimp; cook 2 to 4 minutes, stirring occasionally, until pink. Remove shrimp from skillet; keep warm.

2 In same skillet, heat coconut milk and water to boiling. Break up noodles from soup mix into coconut milk mixture; stir until slightly softened. Stir in vegetables. Heat to boiling. Reduce heat to medium; cook uncovered 4 to 6 minutes, stirring occasionally, until vegetables are almost crisp-tender.

3 Stir in seasoning packet from soup mix and peanut sauce. Cook about 3 minutes, stirring frequently, until hot. Stir in cilantro and lime peel; stir in shrimp. Sprinkle with red pepper flakes. Garnish with peanuts.

1 Serving: Calories 550; Total Fat 34g (Saturated Fat 21g, Trans Fat 1.5g); Cholesterol 160mg; Sodium 690mg; Total Carbohydrate 35g (Dietary Fiber 5g); Protein 27g **Exchanges:** 1½ Starch, ½ Other Carbohydrate, ½ Vegetable, 3 Very Lean Meat, 6½ Fat **Carbohydrate Choices:** 2

salmon with soba noodles and sugar snaps

prep time: 45 Minutes ‖ start to finish: 45 Minutes ‖ 4 servings

1 tablespoon sesame oil

1 tablespoon finely chopped fresh gingerroot

2 cloves garlic, finely chopped

¼ cup honey

4 cups water

½ cup reduced-sodium soy sauce

6 green onions, sliced diagonally, white and green parts separated

2 carrots, cut into matchstick pieces (about 1 cup)

1 lb skinless salmon, cut into 1-inch cubes

6 oz uncooked soba (buckwheat) noodles

1 box (9 oz) frozen sugar snap peas

1 tablespoon lime juice

1 In 5-quart Dutch oven or saucepan, beat oil, gingerroot, garlic and honey with whisk. Beat in water and soy sauce. Heat to boiling over high heat.

2 Add white parts of green onions, the carrots and salmon; return to boiling. Reduce heat to low and simmer 2 minutes, then increase heat to high. Add noodles; heat to a simmer. Reduce heat to medium; cook 6 minutes longer.

3 Meanwhile, microwave frozen sugar snap peas as directed on box 3½ minutes; let stand 1 minute. Stir into noodle mixture. Cover; remove from heat, and let stand 1 minute.

4 Stir in lime juice; top with green parts of green onions, and serve.

1 Serving: Calories 510; Total Fat 16g (Saturated Fat 3g, Trans Fat 0g); Cholesterol 65mg; Sodium 1230mg; Total Carbohydrate 58g (Dietary Fiber 7g); Protein 33g **Exchanges:** 3 Starch, ½ Other Carbohydrate, 1 Vegetable, 3 Lean Meat, 1 Fat **Carbohydrate Choices:** 4

Quick Variation Trade angel hair pasta for soba noodles in a pinch.

buttery fish and vegetables

prep time: **25 Minutes** ‖ start to finish: **25 Minutes** ‖ **4 servings**

2 **tablespoons butter**

1 **cup sliced leeks**

1 **cup shredded carrots (from 10-oz bag)**

1 **lb cod fillets, cut into 4 serving pieces**

1 **can (11 oz) vacuum-packed whole kernel corn or whole kernel corn with red and green peppers, drained**

   Lemon wedges, if desired

1 In 10-inch skillet, melt butter over medium-high heat. Add leeks and carrots; cook 3 minutes, stirring frequently, until softened.

2 Arrange vegetable mixture into 4 mounds in skillet. Place 1 piece of fish on each mound. Pour corn over fish. Reduce heat to medium-low; cover and cook 10 minutes or until fish flakes easily with fork. Serve with lemon wedges.

1 Serving: Calories 200; Total Fat 7g (Saturated Fat 4g, Trans Fat 0g); Cholesterol 75mg; Sodium 550mg; Total Carbohydrate 10g (Dietary Fiber 2g); Protein 23g **Exchanges:** ½ Starch, 3 Very Lean Meat, 1 Fat **Carbohydrate Choices:** ½

Quick Variation Snapper, grouper or any fish with mild flavor and medium-firm to firm texture can be used instead of the cod.

salmon with basil and julienne vegetables

prep time: **15 Minutes** || start to finish: **25 Minutes** || **4 servings**

1   **tablespoon butter**

1   **bag (1 lb) frozen bell pepper and onion stir-fry**

1   **medium zucchini, cut into julienne (matchstick-size) strips**

4   **salmon fillets (4 to 5 oz each)**

2   **tablespoons chopped fresh basil leaves**

½   **teaspoon seasoned salt**

1   **teaspoon lemon-pepper seasoning**

¼   **cup chicken broth**

1 In 12-inch nonstick skillet, melt butter over medium heat. Add bell pepper stir-fry; cook and stir 2 minutes. Stir in zucchini.

2 Place salmon, skin side down, in skillet, pushing down into vegetables if necessary. Sprinkle salmon and vegetables with basil, seasoned salt and lemon-pepper seasoning. Pour broth over salmon and vegetables.

3 Reduce heat to medium-low; cover and cook 8 to 10 minutes or until salmon flakes easily with fork. Using slotted spoon, remove salmon and vegetables from skillet.

1 Serving: Calories 240; Total Fat 10g (Saturated Fat 3.5g, Trans Fat 0g); Cholesterol 80mg; Sodium 410mg; Total Carbohydrate 11g (Dietary Fiber 2g); Protein 26g **Exchanges:** ½ Starch, 1 Vegetable, 3 Lean Meat **Carbohydrate Choices:** 1

Quick Variation If you don't have the bell pepper stir-fry mixture, use 2 cups mixed cut-up fresh bell peppers and onions.

italian-seasoned tilapia and brown rice

prep time: 15 Minutes || **start to finish:** 1 Hour 15 Minutes || **4 servings**

- 1 teaspoon dried Italian seasoning
- ½ teaspoon salt
- ½ teaspoon paprika
- ¼ teaspoon pepper
- 1 tablespoon olive oil
- 1 large onion, chopped (1 cup)
- 2 cloves garlic, finely chopped
- 1 cup vegetable or chicken broth (from 32-oz carton)
- ½ cup dry white wine
- ½ cup uncooked regular long-grain brown rice
- 2 cups frozen mixed vegetables (from 12-oz bag)
- 2 fresh tilapia fillets (about 1 lb), cut in half lengthwise

1 In small bowl, mix Italian seasoning, salt, paprika and pepper; set aside.

2 In 10-inch nonstick skillet, heat oil over medium heat. Add onion and garlic; cook and stir 3 minutes. Stir in broth, wine, rice and 1½ teaspoons of the seasoning mixture. Heat to boiling. Reduce heat; cover and simmer 45 minutes.

3 Stir in frozen vegetables. Heat to boiling. Sprinkle fish with remaining seasoning mixture. Arrange fish over rice and vegetables. Cover; simmer 6 to 10 minutes or until fish flakes easily with fork. Remove from heat; let stand covered 5 minutes or until liquid in rice mixture is absorbed.

1 Serving: Calories 270; Total Fat 7g (Saturated Fat 1.5g, Trans Fat 0g); Cholesterol 50mg; Sodium 600mg; Total Carbohydrate 26g (Dietary Fiber 4g); Protein 26g **Exchanges:** 1½ Starch, 1 Vegetable, 3 Very Lean Meat, 1 Fat **Carbohydrate Choices:** 2

Quick Variation If you can't get 2 fillets that equal about 1 pound, feel free to cut what you can get into 1½-inch pieces instead.

creamy tuna primavera

prep time: **15 Minutes** || start to finish: **20 Minutes** || **5 servings**

1¾ cups milk

1½ cups hot water

3 tablespoons butter

1 box creamy broccoli and pasta skillet meal mix

2 medium carrots, cut into ⅛-inch slices (1 cup)

2 cans (5 oz each) tuna, drained

1 cup frozen sweet peas, thawed, drained

1 jar (4.5 oz) sliced mushrooms, drained, if desired

1 In 12-inch skillet, heat milk, hot water, butter, uncooked pasta and sauce mix (from skillet meal mix), carrots and tuna to boiling over high heat, stirring occasionally.

2 Reduce heat; cover and simmer 5 minutes, stirring occasionally.

3 Stir in peas and mushrooms. Cover; simmer about 5 minutes or until vegetables are tender. Remove from heat; let stand covered 5 minutes (sauce will thicken as it stands).

1 Serving: Calories 230; Total Fat 9g (Saturated Fat 6g, Trans Fat 0g); Cholesterol 40mg; Sodium 450mg; Total Carbohydrate 16g (Dietary Fiber 2g); Protein 20g **Exchanges:** 1 Starch, ½ Vegetable, 2½ Lean Meat **Carbohydrate Choices:** 1

time-saver Tuna is often available in handy pouches. The pouches are really easy to use, as no draining is required.

easy italian skillet supper

prep time: **20 Minutes** || start to finish: **30 Minutes** || **4 servings**

1 can (14 oz) vegetable broth

1¼ cups uncooked orzo or rosamarina pasta (8 oz)

1 can (14.5 oz) diced tomatoes with basil, garlic and oregano, undrained

1 can (15 oz) black beans, drained, rinsed

2 cups frozen broccoli, cauliflower and carrots (from 1-lb bag)

2 tablespoons chopped fresh parsley, if desired

2 tablespoons shredded Parmesan cheese

1 In 10-inch skillet, heat broth to boiling. Stir in pasta. Return to boiling. Reduce heat to low; cover and simmer 10 to 12 minutes or until liquid is absorbed.

2 Stir in tomatoes, beans and vegetables. Cover; cook over medium heat 5 to 10 minutes, stirring occasionally, until vegetables are tender.

3 Stir in parsley; sprinkle with cheese.

1 Serving: Calories 370; Total Fat 3g (Saturated Fat 1g, Trans Fat 0g); Cholesterol 0mg; Sodium 940mg; Total Carbohydrate 67g (Dietary Fiber 16g); Protein 18g **Exchanges:** 4 Starch, 1 Vegetable, ½ Lean Meat **Carbohydrate Choices:** 4½

barley and black bean pilaf

prep time: 40 Minutes || **start to finish:** 1 Hour 20 Minutes || 6 servings (1⅓ cups each)

1 tablespoon vegetable oil

1 large onion, chopped (1 cup)

2 cloves garlic, finely chopped

1 carton (32 oz) reduced-sodium chicken broth

1 cup uncooked medium pearled barley

½ teaspoon ground turmeric

½ teaspoon ground cumin

½ teaspoon ground chipotle chile powder

½ teaspoon salt

8 pattypan squash, cut into fourths, or 2 medium yellow summer squash, cut in half lengthwise, then crosswise into ½-inch slices

1 large red bell pepper, coarsely chopped (1½ cups)

1 can (15 oz) black beans, drained, rinsed

1 cup frozen sweet peas

1 In 12-inch nonstick skillet, heat oil over medium heat. Add onion and garlic; cook 4 minutes, stirring occasionally.

2 Stir in broth, barley, turmeric, cumin, chile powder and salt. Heat to boiling. Reduce heat; cover and simmer 40 minutes, stirring occasionally.

3 Stir in squash, bell pepper and beans. Cover; cook 10 to 15 minutes, stirring occasionally, until squash and barley are just tender.

4 Stir in peas. Cover; cook 3 to 5 minutes longer or until peas are cooked. Let stand covered 5 to 10 minutes to let flavors blend before serving.

1 Serving: Calories 280; Total Fat 3.5g (Saturated Fat 0.5g, Trans Fat 0g); Cholesterol 0mg; Sodium 570mg; Total Carbohydrate 50g (Dietary Fiber 13g); Protein 12g
Exchanges: 1½ Starch, ½ Other Carbohydrate, 1 Vegetable, 1 Very Lean Meat, ½ Fat
Carbohydrate Choices: 3

Quick Variations Turn this dish into a shrimp main dish by adding 1 pound of shrimp with the peas. Choose frozen cooked shrimp that have been peeled and deveined with the tail shells removed. Thaw them in a strainer under running cold water. It will only take a few minutes before they're ready to add to the skillet.

To make this recipe meatless, use vegetable broth in place of chicken broth.

CHAPTER
5

slow-
cooker
choices

chicken and barley risotto with edamame

prep time: 25 Minutes || start to finish: 4 Hours 55 Minutes || 9 servings (1 cup each)

1¼ lb boneless skinless chicken breasts, cut into ¾-inch cubes

3 medium onions, chopped (1½ cups)

1¼ cups uncooked pearl barley

½ cup shredded carrot

2 cloves garlic, finely chopped

½ teaspoon salt

½ teaspoon dried thyme leaves

1 carton (32 oz) chicken broth

1 cup frozen shelled edamame (from 10-oz bag), thawed

½ cup shredded Parmesan cheese (2 oz)

1 Spray 4- to 5-quart slow cooker with cooking spray. In slow cooker, mix chicken, onions, barley, carrot, garlic, salt, thyme and 3 cups of the broth.

2 Cover; cook on Low heat setting 4 to 5 hours.

3 In 2-cup microwavable measuring cup, microwave remaining 1 cup broth uncovered on High 2 to 3 minutes or until boiling. Stir thawed edamame and boiling broth into chicken mixture in slow cooker.

4 Increase heat setting to High; cover and cook 25 to 30 minutes longer or until edamame are tender. Stir in cheese.

1 Serving: Calories 250; Total Fat 6g (Saturated Fat 2g, Trans Fat 0g); Cholesterol 45mg; Sodium 690mg; Total Carbohydrate 27g (Dietary Fiber 6g); Protein 23g **Exchanges:** 1½ Starch, 1 Vegetable, 2 Lean Meat **Carbohydrate Choices:** 2

Quick Variation To turn this into a meatless meal, omit the chicken and use vegetable broth instead of chicken broth.

african groundnut stew with chicken

prep time: 20 Minutes ‖ **start to finish:** 8 Hours 20 Minutes ‖ 8 servings (1½ cups each)

6 **boneless skinless chicken thighs (about 1 lb)**

3 **boneless skinless chicken breasts (about 12 oz)**

1 **large onion, chopped (1 cup)**

¾ **cup peanut butter**

1 **can (28 oz) diced tomatoes, undrained**

1¾ **cups chicken broth (from 32-oz carton)**

2 **tablespoons grated fresh gingerroot**

2 **tablespoons tomato paste**

2 **teaspoons curry powder**

1 **teaspoon crushed red pepper flakes**

½ **teaspoon salt**

1½ **lb dark-orange sweet potatoes (3 medium), peeled, cubed (about 4 cups)**

1 **lb small red potatoes, cut into eighths (about 3 cups)**

1 Spray 5- to 6-quart slow cooker with cooking spray. In slow cooker, layer all ingredients in order listed, spooning peanut butter in dollops.

2 Cover; cook on Low heat setting 8 to 10 hours.

3 Before serving, break up chicken.

1 Serving: Calories 420; Total Fat 19g (Saturated Fat 4.5g, Trans Fat 0g); Cholesterol 60mg; Sodium 710mg; Total Carbohydrate 32g (Dietary Fiber 6g); Protein 31g **Exchanges:** 1½ Starch, ½ Other Carbohydrate, 1 Vegetable, 3½ Lean Meat, 1 Fat **Carbohydrate Choices:** 2

Quick Variation We like the combination of chicken thighs and breasts in this recipe, but you can choose to use all chicken thighs instead.

spicy chicken and sausage soup

prep time: 20 Minutes ‖ **start to finish:** 8 Hours 35 Minutes ‖ 6 servings (1⅓ cups each)

1¼ lb boneless skinless chicken thighs, cubed

1 can (14.5 oz) diced tomatoes, undrained

1¾ cups chicken broth (from 32-oz carton)

1 cup water

½ teaspoon red pepper sauce

8 oz cooked kielbasa, sliced

1 cup frozen bell pepper and onion stir-fry (from 1-lb bag), thawed

½ cup uncooked instant white rice

1 Spray 3- to 3½-quart slow cooker with cooking spray. In slow cooker, mix chicken, tomatoes, broth, water and pepper sauce.

2 Cover; cook on Low heat setting 8 to 10 hours.

3 Stir in kielbasa, stir-fry vegetables and rice. Increase heat setting to High; cover and cook 10 to 15 minutes longer or until rice is tender.

1 Serving: Calories 330; Total Fat 19g (Saturated Fat 6g, Trans Fat 0g); Cholesterol 80mg; Sodium 810mg; Total Carbohydrate 14g (Dietary Fiber 1g); Protein 27g **Exchanges:** ½ Starch, 1 Vegetable, 3½ Lean Meat, 1½ Fat **Carbohydrate Choices:** 1

Quick Variation Season this soup to suit your family. For a spicier flavor, increase the amount of pepper sauce. Also, any cooked spicy sausage can be used — try turkey kielbasa or smoked sausage for a change of flavor.

italian chicken-lentil soup

prep time: 15 Minutes || **start to finish:** 5 Hours 30 Minutes || 6 servings

4	medium carrots, sliced (2 cups)
1	medium zucchini, chopped (2 cups)
1	medium onion, chopped (½ cup)
1	cup dried lentils (8 oz), sorted, rinsed
4½	cups chicken broth (from two 32-oz cartons)
½	teaspoon salt
¼	teaspoon pepper
1	lb boneless skinless chicken thighs, trimmed of excess fat
1	can (28 oz) diced tomatoes, undrained
1	cup sliced fresh mushrooms (3 oz)
¼	cup chopped fresh or 1 tablespoon dried basil leaves
	Shredded Parmesan cheese, if desired

1 Spray 3½- to 6-quart slow cooker with cooking spray. In slow cooker, mix carrots, zucchini, onion, lentils, broth, salt and pepper; top with chicken.

2 Cover; cook on Low heat setting 5 to 6 hours.

3 Transfer chicken from slow cooker to cutting board. Use 2 forks to pull chicken into shreds. Return chicken to slow cooker. Stir in tomatoes and mushrooms. Cover; cook about 15 minutes or until thoroughly heated. Sprinkle with basil. Serve with cheese.

1 Serving: Calories 280; Total Fat 4g (Saturated Fat 1g, Trans Fat 0g); Cholesterol 30mg; Sodium 1200mg; Total Carbohydrate 35g (Dietary Fiber 10g); Protein 25g **Exchanges:** 2 Starch, 1 Vegetable, 2½ Very Lean Meat **Carbohydrate Choices:** 2

turkey–butternut squash ragout

prep time: **15 Minutes** || start to finish: **7 Hours 15 Minutes** || **4 servings**

1½ lb turkey thighs (about 2 medium), skin removed

1 small butternut squash (about 2 lb), peeled, seeded and cut into 1½-inch pieces (3 cups)

1 medium onion, cut in half, sliced

1 can (16 oz) baked beans, undrained

1 can (14.5 oz) diced tomatoes with Italian seasonings, undrained

2 tablespoons chopped fresh parsley

1 Spray 3- to 4-quart slow cooker with cooking spray. In slow cooker, mix all ingredients except parsley.

2 Cover; cook on Low heat setting 7 to 8 hours.

3 Remove turkey from slow cooker; place on cutting board. Remove meat from bones; discard bones. Return turkey to slow cooker; stir to combine. Just before serving, sprinkle with parsley.

1 Serving: Calories 380; Total Fat 6g (Saturated Fat 2g, Trans Fat 0g); Cholesterol 115mg; Sodium 730mg; Total Carbohydrate 46g (Dietary Fiber 10g); Protein 36g **Exchanges:** 3 Starch, 1 Vegetable, 3 Very Lean Meat **Carbohydrate Choices:** 3

healthy twist Butternut squash, rich in color and great flavor, is an excellent source of vitamin A.

herbed turkey and wild rice casserole

prep time: 15 Minutes || **start to finish:** 6 Hours 45 Minutes || 6 servings

6 slices bacon, cut into ½-inch pieces

1 lb turkey breast tenderloins, cut into ¾-inch pieces

1 medium onion, chopped (½ cup)

1 medium carrot, sliced (½ cup)

1 medium stalk celery, sliced (½ cup)

2 cans (14 oz each) chicken broth (4 cups)

1 can (10¾ oz) condensed cream of chicken soup

¼ teaspoon dried marjoram leaves

⅛ teaspoon pepper

1¼ cups uncooked wild rice, rinsed, drained

1 In 10-inch skillet, cook bacon over medium heat, stirring occasionally, until crisp. Stir in turkey. Cook 3 to 5 minutes, stirring occasionally, until turkey is browned. Stir in onion, carrot and celery. Cook 2 minutes longer, stirring occasionally; drain.

2 Spray 3½- to 6-quart slow cooker with cooking spray. In slow cooker, beat 1 can of the broth and the soup with whisk until smooth. Stir in remaining can of broth, the marjoram and pepper. Stir in turkey mixture and wild rice.

3 Cover; cook on High heat setting 30 minutes.

4 Reduce heat setting to Low; cover and cook 6 to 7 hours longer or until rice is tender and liquid is absorbed.

1 Serving: Calories 340; Total Fat 9g (Saturated Fat 2.5g, Trans Fat 0g); Cholesterol 65mg; Sodium 1190mg; Total Carbohydrate 36g (Dietary Fiber 3g); Protein 30g **Exchanges:** 2 Starch, 1 Vegetable, 3 Very Lean Meat, 1 Fat **Carbohydrate Choices:** 2½

turkey breast with sweet potatoes

prep time: 25 Minutes ‖ **start to finish:** 7 Hours 25 Minutes ‖ 8 servings

1 bone-in turkey breast (4 to 5 lb), thawed if frozen

2 or 3 dark-orange sweet potatoes, peeled, cut into 1-inch pieces

1 cup frozen pearl onions (from 1-lb bag), thawed

½ cup chicken broth

¼ cup orange marmalade

2 tablespoons balsamic vinegar

½ teaspoon salt

½ teaspoon dried marjoram leaves

2 cloves garlic, finely chopped

2 tablespoons cornstarch

2 tablespoons water

1 Spray 5- to 6-quart slow cooker with cooking spray. Place turkey in slow cooker. Arrange sweet potatoes and onions around turkey. In small bowl, mix remaining ingredients except cornstarch and water; pour over turkey and vegetables.

2 Cover; cook on Low heat setting 7 to 8 hours.

3 Remove turkey and vegetables from slow cooker; cover to keep warm. If desired, skim fat from juices in slow cooker. Pour juices into 4-cup microwavable measuring cup. In small bowl, mix cornstarch and water until smooth; stir into juices in cup. Microwave uncovered on High 2 to 3 minutes, stirring every minute, until mixture thickens. Serve with turkey and vegetables.

1 Serving: Calories 360; Total Fat 12g (Saturated Fat 3.5g, Trans Fat 0g); Cholesterol 115mg; Sodium 320mg; Total Carbohydrate 20g (Dietary Fiber 2g); Protein 44g **Exchanges:** 1 Starch, 6 Very Lean Meat, 1½ Fat **Carbohydrate Choices:** 1

healthy twist You can reduce the fat to about 2 grams and the calories to about 280 per serving by removing the skin from the turkey before cooking.

Heirloom Recipe and New Twist

family-favorite chili

prep time: 20 Minutes ‖ **start to finish:** 6 Hours 40 Minutes ‖ 8 servings

- 2 lb lean (at least 80%) ground beef
- 1 large onion, chopped (1 cup)
- 2 cloves garlic, finely chopped
- 1 can (28 oz) diced tomatoes, undrained
- 1 can (15 oz) tomato sauce
- 2 tablespoons chili powder
- 1½ teaspoons ground cumin
- ½ teaspoon salt
- ½ teaspoon pepper
- 1 can (15 to 16 oz) kidney or pinto beans, drained, rinsed

    Shredded Cheddar cheese, if desired

1 In 12-inch skillet, cook beef over medium heat 8 to 10 minutes, stirring occasionally, until browned; drain.

2 Spray 3½- to 6-quart slow cooker with cooking spray. In slow cooker, mix beef and remaining ingredients except beans and cheese.

3 Cover; cook on Low heat setting 6 to 8 hours (or High heat setting 3 to 4 hours).

4 Stir in beans. Increase heat setting to High; cover and cook 15 to 20 minutes longer or until slightly thickened. Sprinkle with cheese.

1 Serving: Calories 300; Total Fat 12g (Saturated Fat 4.5g, Trans Fat 0.5g); Cholesterol 70mg; Sodium 800mg; Total Carbohydrate 22g (Dietary Fiber 6g); Protein 27g **Exchanges:** 1 Starch, 1 Vegetable, 3½ Lean Meat **Carbohydrate Choices:** 1½

Quick Variation For an alternative chili, reduce ground beef to 1 pound. Add 1 pound cooked smoked beef sausage, cut into ½-inch slices, in step 2. Substitute shredded smoked Cheddar or smoked Gouda cheese for the shredded Cheddar.

three-chile chunky beef chili

prep time: **20 Minutes** || start to finish: **8 Hours 20 Minutes** || **6 servings (1⅓ cups each)**

- 2 lb boneless beef chuck roast, cut into 1-inch cubes
- 1 large onion, chopped (1 cup)
- 1 or 2 chipotle chiles in adobo sauce (from 7-oz can), chopped
- 1 ancho chile, cut into small pieces
- 1 tablespoon chili powder
- 1 teaspoon ground cumin
- ½ teaspoon salt
- ½ teaspoon garlic powder
- 2 cans (14.5 oz each) diced tomatoes with green chiles, undrained
- 1 can (15 oz) black beans, drained, rinsed

1 Spray 3- to 4-quart slow cooker with cooking spray. In slow cooker, mix all ingredients.

2 Cover; cook on Low heat setting 8 to 10 hours (or on High heat setting 4 to 5 hours).

1 Serving: Calories 420; Total Fat 17g (Saturated Fat 6g, Trans Fat 0.5g); Cholesterol 80mg; Sodium 1010mg; Total Carbohydrate 30g (Dietary Fiber 11g); Protein 37g **Exchanges:** 1½ Starch, ½ Other Carbohydrate, ½ Vegetable, 4½ Lean Meat, ½ Fat **Carbohydrate Choices:** 2

time-saver Spraying the slow cooker with cooking spray before adding the ingredients makes for easy cleanup!

asian beef roast with cabbage and pasta

prep time: 30 Minutes ‖ start to finish: 7 Hours 30 Minutes ‖ 6 servings

1 boneless beef chuck roast (3 lb), trimmed of excess fat

1 teaspoon garlic salt

½ teaspoon pepper

1 cup water

½ cup hoisin sauce

¼ cup reduced-sodium soy sauce

2 tablespoons finely chopped fresh gingerroot

1 teaspoon sesame oil

½ teaspoon crushed red pepper flakes

4 medium carrots, cut into 1-inch pieces

½ head cabbage, cut into 6 wedges

6 oz uncooked angel hair pasta

Toasted sesame seed, chopped bell pepper (any color) and sliced green onions, if desired

1 Spray 5- to 6-quart slow cooker with cooking spray. Sprinkle beef with ½ teaspoon of the garlic salt and the pepper. Pour water into slow cooker; place beef in center.

2 In small bowl, stir together hoisin sauce, soy sauce, gingerroot, sesame oil, red pepper and remaining ½ teaspoon garlic salt. Pour over top and sides of beef. Arrange carrots around beef. Arrange cabbage wedges in single layer on top of beef and carrots.

3 Cover; cook on Low heat setting 7 to 8 hours.

4 Increase heat setting to High. Using slotted spoon, transfer vegetables from slow cooker to serving bowl; cover with foil. Transfer beef from slow cooker to cutting board; cover with foil. Let stand 5 minutes before cutting beef.

5 Meanwhile, break pasta in half; add to sauce in slow cooker, pushing pasta below surface of sauce. Cover; cook on High heat setting 9 to 11 minutes or until pasta is tender.

6 Cut beef across grain into slices. Serve beef, pasta and vegetables with any remaining sauce. Garnish with sesame seed, bell pepper and green onions.

1 Serving: Calories 590; Total Fat 26g (Saturated Fat 10g, Trans Fat 1g); Cholesterol 145mg; Sodium 980mg; Total Carbohydrate 40g (Dietary Fiber 3g); Protein 48g **Exchanges:** 2 Starch, 2 Vegetable, 5½ Lean Meat, 1½ Fat **Carbohydrate Choices:** 2½

time-saver This meal can be cooked on the High heat setting, and it'll be on the table in 3½ to 4½ hours.

old-world corned beef and vegetables

prep time: 15 Minutes ‖ **start to finish:** 8 Hours 15 Minutes ‖ 10 servings

2½ pounds medium new potatoes, (about 8), cut in half

2 cups baby-cut carrots

1 cup frozen small whole onions, thawed

1 corned beef brisket (3 to 3½ lb), trimmed of fat

⅛ teaspoon pepper

½ cup water

1 tablespoon Worcestershire sauce

1 tablespoon cornstarch

2 tablespoons cold water

1 Spray 4- to 6-quart slow cooker with cooking spray. Mix potatoes, carrots and onions in slow cooker.

2 Thoroughly rinse corned beef; discard seasoning packet. Place beef on vegetables; sprinkle with pepper. Mix ½ cup water and the Worcestershire sauce; pour over beef.

3 Cover; cook on low heat setting 8 to 9 hours.

4 Remove beef and vegetables from slow cooker; cover to keep warm. Pour juices from slow cooker into 1-quart saucepan; heat to boiling. In small bowl, mix cornstarch and cold water until smooth; stir into juices. Cook, stirring constantly, until sauce has thickened. Serve sauce with beef and vegetables.

1 Serving: Calories 350; Total Fat 19g (Saturated Fat 6g, Trans Fat 1g); Cholesterol 95mg; Sodium 1140mg; Total Carbohydrate 26g (Dietary Fiber 3g); Protein 19g **Exchanges:** 1 Starch, 2 Vegetable, 2 Medium-Fat Meat, 1½ Fat **Carbohydrate Choices:** 2

Quick Variation Cut a small head of cabbage into 6 wedges, and place on top of the corned beef in the slow cooker before cooking.

cranberry corned beef

5 large carrots, cut into 3-inch pieces

1 large onion, cut into 6 wedges

1 corned beef brisket with spice packet (4 lb), trimmed of fat

1 can (14 oz) whole berry cranberry sauce

1 can (14 oz) jellied cranberry sauce

1 box (2 oz) onion soup mix (2 packages)

½ cup sour cream

4 teaspoons prepared horseradish

2 tablespoons chopped fresh parsley, if desired

¼ teaspoon pepper

1 Spray 5-quart slow cooker with cooking spray. In slow cooker, place carrots and onion. Top with beef. Sprinkle with spices from packet. In medium bowl, mix both cranberry sauces and the soup mix; spoon over beef.

2 Cover; cook on High heat setting 1 hour. Reduce heat setting to Low; cook 8 hours longer or until beef is tender.

3 Meanwhile, in small bowl, mix sour cream and horseradish until blended. Cover; refrigerate until serving time.

4 Remove beef from slow cooker; place on serving platter. Cut beef across grain into thin slices. Spoon carrots and onion around beef. If desired, drizzle with cooking liquid. Sprinkle with parsley and pepper. Serve with horseradish sauce.

1 Serving: Calories 630; Total Fat 34g (Saturated Fat 12g, Trans Fat 1.5g); Cholesterol 165mg; Sodium 2520mg; Total Carbohydrate 51g (Dietary Fiber 3g); Protein 30g **Exchanges:** 1 Fruit, 2½ Other Carbohydrate, 4 Medium-Fat Meat, 3 Fat **Carbohydrate Choices:** 3½

colombian beef and sweet potato stew

prep time: 15 Minutes ‖ **start to finish:** 8 Hours 15 Minutes ‖ 6 servings

1 lb boneless beef chuck flatiron steak, trimmed of excess fat, cut into 1-inch pieces

½ teaspoon salt

¼ teaspoon pepper

1 teaspoon olive or vegetable oil

3 cups 1-inch pieces peeled sweet potatoes

2 teaspoons finely chopped garlic

2 whole cloves

1 dried bay leaf

1 cinnamon stick

1 large onion, cut into eighths

1 can (28 oz) Italian-style tomatoes, undrained

8 dried apricots, cut in half

Chopped fresh parsley, if desired

1 Sprinkle beef with salt and pepper. In 10-inch skillet, heat oil over medium-high heat. Add beef; cook about 5 minutes, stirring occasionally, until browned.

2 Spray 4- to 5-quart slow cooker with cooking spray. In slow cooker, mix beef and remaining ingredients except apricots and parsley.

3 Cover; cook on Low heat setting 8 hours.

4 Stir in apricots. Cover; cook on Low heat setting about 15 minutes longer or until apricots are tender. Remove and discard cloves, bay leaf and cinnamon stick. Sprinkle stew with parsley.

1 Serving: Calories 260; Total Fat 9g (Saturated Fat 3.5g, Trans Fat 0g); Cholesterol 40mg; Sodium 630mg; Total Carbohydrate 27g (Dietary Fiber 5g); Protein 17g **Exchanges:** ½ Starch, 1 Other Carbohydrate, 1 Vegetable, 2 Lean Meat, ½ Fat **Carbohydrate Choices:** 2

time-saver To save a bit of time, purchase already cut-up beef stew meat instead of the boneless beef chuck.

caramelized onion beef stew

prep time: 35 Minutes ‖ **start to finish:** 8 Hours 50 Minutes ‖ 6 servings

2 tablespoons butter

4 cups halved and thinly sliced sweet onions (about 1½ onions)

2 teaspoons sugar

2 teaspoons chopped fresh thyme leaves

1½ lb beef stew meat

1 cup beef broth (from 32-oz carton)

1 package (0.87 oz) onion gravy mix

2 cups 1-inch pieces diagonally cut carrots

1 cup 1-inch pieces diagonally cut parsnips

½ cup frozen sweet peas

1 Spray 5 to 6-quart slow cooker with cooking spray. In 10-inch skillet, melt butter over medium-low heat. Cook onions and sugar in butter 30 to 35 minutes, stirring frequently, until onions are deep golden brown and caramelized. Stir in thyme and stew meat; place in slow cooker.

2 In medium bowl, mix broth and gravy mix; pour over meat mixture in slow cooker. Top with carrots and parsnips. Cover; cook on Low heat setting 8 to 9 hours or until beef and vegetables are tender.

3 Stir in peas. Cover; cook 10 to 15 minutes longer or until hot.

1 Serving: Calories 290; Total Fat 15g (Saturated Fat 6g, Trans Fat 0.5g); Cholesterol 60mg; Total Carbohydrate 21g (Dietary Fiber 4g); Protein 18g%
Exchanges: 1 Starch, 1 Vegetable, 2 Lean Meat, 1½ Fat **Carbohydrate Choices:** 1½

Quick Variation Substitute mushroom beef gravy mix or brown beef gravy mix for the onion gravy mix, if you like.

lentil and canadian bacon soup

prep time: **20 Minutes** || start to finish: **8 Hours 20 Minutes** || **8 servings**

1 **bag (1 lb) dried lentils (2 cups), sorted, rinsed**

4 **cups water**

3½ **cups vegetable broth (from 32-oz carton)**

1 **package (6 oz) sliced Canadian bacon, coarsely chopped**

2 **medium carrots, cut into ½-inch pieces (1 cup)**

1 **medium potato, peeled, cut into ½-inch pieces (1 cup)**

1 **medium onion, chopped (½ cup)**

1 **medium stalk celery, cut into ½-inch pieces (½ cup)**

1 **teaspoon dried thyme leaves**

½ **teaspoon salt**

¼ **teaspoon black pepper**

1 Spray 3½- to 6-quart slow cooker with cooking spray. In slow cooker, mix all ingredients.

2 Cover; cook on Low heat setting 8 to 9 hours (or High heat setting 3 to 5 hours) or until lentils are tender. Stir well before serving.

1 Serving: Calories 260; Total Fat 2.5g (Saturated Fat 0.5g, Trans Fat 0g); Cholesterol 10mg; Sodium 910mg; Total Carbohydrate 39g (Dietary Fiber 10g); Protein 20g **Exchanges:** 2 Starch, 2 Vegetable, 1 Lean Meat **Carbohydrate Choices:** 2½

Quick Variation Canadian bacon is a closer relative to ham than to regular bacon. It's lean and fully cooked. If you prefer ham, use 1½ cups chopped cooked ham instead of the Canadian bacon.

cheesy potato-bacon soup

prep time: 15 Minutes || **start to finish:** 6 Hours 45 Minutes || 6 servings (1½ cups each)

1 bag (32 oz) frozen southern-style diced hash brown potatoes, thawed

1 medium onion, chopped (½ cup)

1 medium stalk celery, diced (½ cup)

3½ cups chicken broth (from 32-oz carton)

1 cup water

3 tablespoons all-purpose flour

1 cup half-and-half

2 cups shredded Cheddar cheese (8 oz)

12 slices bacon, crisply cooked, crumbled

4 medium green onions, thinly sliced (¼ cup)

1 Spray 3- to 4-quart slow cooker with cooking spray. In slow cooker, mix potatoes, onion, celery, broth and water.

2 Cover; cook on Low heat setting 6 to 8 hours.

3 In small bowl, mix flour and half-and-half; stir into potato mixture. Increase heat setting to High; cover and cook 20 to 30 minutes longer or until mixture thickens.

4 Stir in cheese until melted. Stir in half of the bacon. Sprinkle each serving with remaining bacon and green onions.

1 Serving: Calories 410; Total Fat 15g (Saturated Fat 9g, Trans Fat 0g); Cholesterol 45mg; Sodium 1210mg; Total Carbohydrate 50g (Dietary Fiber 5g); Protein 19g **Exchanges:** 3½ Starch, 1 High-Fat Meat, 1 Fat **Carbohydrate Choices:** 3

Quick Variation Make this an easy meatless choice — just omit the bacon pieces and use vegetable broth instead of the chicken broth.

easy bean and kielbasa soup

prep time: 15 Minutes || **start to finish:** 8 Hours 30 Minutes || **8 servings**

1¼ cups mixed dried bean soup mix

1 ring (1 lb) fully cooked kielbasa, cut in half lengthwise, then crosswise into slices

4 medium carrots, chopped (2 cups)

3 medium stalks celery, chopped (1½ cups)

1 large onion, chopped (1 cup)

5 cans (14 oz each) chicken broth

2 tablespoons tomato paste

1 teaspoon dried thyme leaves

½ teaspoon salt

½ teaspoon pepper

1 can (14.5 oz) diced tomatoes, undrained

1 Spray 5- to 6-quart slow cooker with cooking spray. In slow cooker, mix all ingredients except tomatoes.

2 Cover; cook on Low heat setting 8 to 10 hours or until vegetables are tender.

3 Stir in tomatoes. Increase heat setting to High. Cover; cook about 15 minutes longer or until hot.

1 Serving: Calories 370; Total Fat 18g (Saturated Fat 6g, Trans Fat 0.5g); Cholesterol 35mg; Sodium 2020mg; Total Carbohydrate 35g (Dietary Fiber 6g); Protein 18g **Exchanges:** 2 Starch, 1 Vegetable, 1½ High-Fat Meat, 1 Fat **Carbohydrate Choices:** 2

golden pea and ham soup

prep time: **10 Minutes** || start to finish: **8 Hours 40 Minutes** || **5 servings (1½ cups each)**

1 bag (1 lb) yellow split peas, sorted, rinsed

1 cup julienne-cut carrots (from 10-oz bag)

8 oz cooked ham, chopped (1⅓ cups)

½ teaspoon dried thyme leaves

½ teaspoon dried marjoram leaves

¼ teaspoon pepper

2 cans (14 oz each) chicken broth

1½ cups water

1 In 3- to 4-quart slow cooker, mix all ingredients.

2 Cover; cook on Low heat setting 8 to 10 hours.

3 Increase heat setting to High; stir well. Cover; cook 30 minutes longer.

1 Serving: Calories 390; Total Fat 6g (Saturated Fat 2g, Trans Fat 0g); Cholesterol 25mg; Sodium 1410mg; Total Carbohydrate 51g (Dietary Fiber 25g); Protein 33g **Exchanges:** 3½ Starch, 3 Very Lean Meat, ½ Fat **Carbohydrate Choices:** 3½

time-saver Look for diced cooked ham at the cooked meat counter of the grocery store.

pork chops with vegetable medley

prep time: **20 Minutes** ‖ start to finish: **3 Hours 35 Minutes** ‖ **4 servings**

1½ teaspoons seasoned salt

1 teaspoon garlic-pepper blend

4 boneless pork loin chops, ½ inch thick (about 1 lb)

2 tablespoons olive oil

1 cup ready-to-eat baby-cut carrots

4 small red potatoes, cut in half

1 medium onion, cut into thin wedges

1 small yellow summer squash, thinly sliced

¼ cup chopped fresh basil leaves

1 In very small bowl, mix salt and garlic-pepper blend. Sprinkle half of seasoning mixture over pork chops. In 12-inch skillet, heat 1 tablespoon of the oil over medium-high heat. Add pork chops; cook about 4 minutes, turning once, just until browned.

2 Spray 4- to 5-quart slow cooker with cooking spray. Place pork chops in slow cooker; top with carrots, potatoes and onion.

3 Cover; cook on Low heat setting 3 to 4 hours.

4 In medium bowl, mix squash, basil, remaining 1 tablespoon oil and remaining half of seasoning mixture; spoon on top of vegetable mixture in slow cooker.

5 Increase heat setting to High; cover and cook 10 to 15 minutes longer or until squash is crisp-tender.

1 Serving: Calories 390; Total Fat 15g (Saturated Fat 4g, Trans Fat 0g); Cholesterol 65mg; Sodium 590mg; Total Carbohydrate 37g (Dietary Fiber 5g); Protein 27g **Exchanges:** 2 Starch, 1½ Vegetable, 2½ Lean Meat, 1½ Fat **Carbohydrate Choices:** 2½

Quick Variation Zucchini can be substituted for the yellow squash. Since it is cooked for a short length of time, it will maintain its bright green color.

maple-sage pork roast

prep time: 30 Minutes || **start to finish:** 8 Hours 30 Minutes || 8 servings

1 boneless pork shoulder roast (2 to 3 lb)

2 tablespoons real maple or maple-flavored syrup

1 clove garlic, finely chopped

2 teaspoons dried sage leaves

½ teaspoon beef bouillon granules

1 cup water

2 cups cubed (1½ inch) peeled butternut squash

2 cups ready-to-eat baby-cut carrots, cut in half lengthwise

2 small onions, cut into wedges

3 tablespoons cornstarch

1 Spray 4- to 5-quart slow cooker with cooking spray. If pork roast comes in netting or is tied, remove netting or strings. Place pork in slow cooker.

2 In small bowl, mix syrup, garlic, sage, bouillon granules and ½ cup of the water; spoon over pork. Arrange squash, carrots and onions around pork.

3 Cover; cook on Low heat setting 8 to 9 hours.

4 Using slotted spoon, transfer pork and vegetables from slow cooker to serving platter; cover to keep warm. If desired, skim fat from cooking liquid. Pour liquid into 4-cup microwavable measuring cup. In small bowl, mix cornstarch and remaining ½ cup water until smooth; stir into liquid. Microwave uncovered on High 2 to 3 minutes, stirring every minute, until mixture thickens. Serve with pork and vegetables.

1 Serving: Calories 280; Total Fat 14g (Saturated Fat 5g, Trans Fat 0g); Cholesterol 75mg; Sodium 120mg; Total Carbohydrate 14g (Dietary Fiber 1g); Protein 25g **Exchanges:** 1 Starch, ½ Vegetable, ½ Very Lean Meat, 2½ Lean Meat, 1 Fat **Carbohydrate Choices:** 1

Quick Variation Whole carrots, quartered lengthwise and then cut crosswise into 2-inch pieces, can be substituted for the baby carrots.

porketta pot roast

prep time: 15 Minutes ‖ **start to finish:** 9 Hours 15 Minutes ‖ 8 servings

2　teaspoons dried Italian seasoning

1½　teaspoons fennel seed, crushed

¾　teaspoon salt

½　teaspoon celery seed

1　boneless pork shoulder (3 lb)

3　medium parsnips, peeled, cut into ¾-inch pieces (3 cups)

2　medium sweet potatoes, peeled, cut into ¾-inch pieces (3 cups)

1½　cloves garlic, cut in half

1½　cups water

1 In small bowl, mix Italian seasoning, fennel seed, salt and celery seed. Pat seasoning mixture evenly onto pork (if pork comes in netting or is tied, do not remove). Heat 12-inch nonstick skillet over medium-high heat. Cook pork in skillet 5 to 10 minutes, turning several times, until browned on all sides.

2 Spray 4- to 5-quart slow cooker with cooking spray. In slow cooker, place parsnips, sweet potatoes and garlic; pour water over vegetables. Place pork on vegetables.

3 Cover; cook on Low heat setting 9 to 10 hours.

4 Remove pork from slow cooker; place on cutting board (remove netting or strings). Cut pork across grain into slices. Serve pork with vegetables and juices.

1 Serving: Calories 350; Total Fat 20g (Saturated Fat 7g, Trans Fat 0g); Cholesterol 90mg; Sodium 290mg; Total Carbohydrate 16g (Dietary Fiber 3g); Protein 26g **Exchanges:** 1 Starch, 3 Medium-Fat Meat, 1 Fat **Carbohydrate Choices:** 1

creamy blue cheese–salmon casserole

prep time: **10 Minutes** || start to finish: **6 Hours 30 Minutes** || **8 servings**

10 to 12 small red potatoes (1½ lb), cut in half

1 lb fresh green beans, trimmed, cut into 1-inch pieces

1 can (15.25 oz) whole kernel sweet corn, drained

1 can (10¾ oz) condensed cream of potato soup

½ cup water

½ teaspoon pepper

½ cup half-and-half

3 tablespoons all-purpose flour

1½ lb salmon fillets, skin removed, cut into bite-size pieces

1 cup crumbled blue cheese (4 oz)

2 tablespoons chopped fresh chives

1 Spray 3- to 4-quart slow cooker with cooking spray. In slow cooker, mix potatoes, beans, corn, soup, water and pepper.

2 Cover; cook on Low heat setting 6 to 7 hours (or on High heat setting 3 hours to 3 hours 30 minutes).

3 In 1-cup measuring cup, mix half-and-half and flour with whisk until well blended. Stir into potato mixture in slow cooker. Stir in salmon. If using Low heat setting, increase to High. Cover; cook 15 to 20 minutes longer or until salmon flakes easily with fork. Stir in cheese and chives.

1 Serving: Calories 460; Total Fat 12g (Saturated Fat 6g, Trans Fat 0g); Cholesterol 75mg; Sodium 580mg; Total Carbohydrate 57g (Dietary Fiber 7g); Protein 29g **Exchanges:** 2½ Starch, ½ Other Carbohydrate, ½ Low-Fat Milk, 1½ Vegetable, 2 Very Lean Meat, 1½ Fat **Carbohydrate Choices:** 4

time-saver Look for salmon fillets that already have the skin removed to save time from having to remove it.

Quick Variation Two cans (7½ ounces each) water-packed chunk-style boneless skinless salmon, drained, can be used instead of the fresh salmon. Since it's already cooked, stir it into the potato mixture and cook about 10 minutes or just until thoroughly heated.

black bean–sweet potato chili

prep time: 35 Minutes || **start to finish:** 7 Hours 35 Minutes || 8 servings

2 large dark-orange sweet potatoes (1½ lb), peeled, cut into ½-inch cubes (about 5 cups)

3 large onions, chopped (3 cups)

3 cloves garlic, finely chopped

2 tablespoons chili powder

1 tablespoon ground cumin

1 can (28 oz) diced tomatoes, undrained

1 can (16 oz) refried black beans

1 can (15 oz) black beans, drained, rinsed

2 cups chicken broth (from 32-oz carton)

2 teaspoons red wine vinegar

Shredded cheese (any variety), if desired

Sour cream, if desired

1 Spray 5- to 6-quart slow cooker with cooking spray. In slow cooker, mix sweet potatoes, onions, garlic, chili powder, cumin, tomatoes, refried beans, black beans and broth.

2 Cover; cook on Low heat setting 7 to 8 hours (or on High heat setting 3½ to 4 hours).

3 Just before serving, stir in vinegar. Serve chili with cheese and sour cream.

1 Serving: Calories 260; Total Fat 2g (Saturated Fat 0.5g, Trans Fat 0g); Cholesterol 0mg; Sodium 900mg; Total Carbohydrate 48g (Dietary Fiber 13g); Protein 12g **Exchanges:** 2½ Other Carbohydrate, 2 Vegetable, 1 Lean Meat **Carbohydrate Choices:** 3

time-saver Make quick work of chopping the garlic and onions by enlisting the help of your food processor. Start by chopping the garlic first, then add the onions and continue chopping. Depending on the size of your food processor, you may need to do the onions in batches. Either way, you save time and tears!

chipotle four-bean chili with lime

prep time: 15 Minutes || **start to finish:** 6 Hours 15 Minutes || 5 servings (1⅓ cups each)

1 medium onion, finely chopped (½ cup)

2 cans (14.5 oz each) diced tomatoes, undrained

1 can (15.5 oz) red beans, drained, rinsed

1 can (15 oz) black beans, drained, rinsed

1 can (15 oz) chickpeas (garbanzo beans), drained, rinsed

1 can (15 oz) pinto beans, drained, rinsed

1 chipotle chile in adobo sauce (from 7-oz can), finely chopped

1 tablespoon dried minced garlic

2 teaspoons ground cumin

2 teaspoons chili powder

2 teaspoons packed brown sugar

½ teaspoon salt

2 tablespoons lime juice

1 Spray 5- to 6-quart slow cooker with cooking spray. In slow cooker, mix all ingredients except lime juice.

2 Cover; cook on Low heat setting 6 to 8 hours (or on High heat setting 2 to 3 hours).

3 Just before serving, stir in lime juice.

1 Serving: Calories 590; Total Fat 4.5g (Saturated Fat 0.5g, Trans Fat 0g); Cholesterol 0mg; Sodium 870mg; Total Carbohydrate 105g (Dietary Fiber 30g); Protein 33g **Exchanges:** 6½ Starch, ½ Vegetable, 1½ Very Lean Meat **Carbohydrate Choices:** 7

Quick Variation Do you prefer one type of bean over others? This dish is colorful and flavorful with the variety of beans, but feel free to substitute one kind of bean for another if you have a preference.

leek and parsnip vegetable stew

prep time: 20 Minutes | **start to finish:** 8 Hours 40 Minutes | 8 servings

4 **medium red potatoes, cut into ½-inch pieces**

2 **medium leeks, cut in half lengthwise, rinsed and cut into ½-inch pieces (4 cups)**

4 **medium stalks celery, cut into ½-inch pieces (2 cups)**

3 **medium carrots, cut into ½-inch pieces (1½ cups)**

2 **medium parsnips, peeled, cut into ½-inch pieces (1½ cups)**

1 **can (28 oz) whole tomatoes, undrained, cut up**

1 **can (14 oz) chicken broth**

½ **teaspoon dried thyme leaves**

½ **teaspoon dried rosemary leaves**

½ **teaspoon salt**

3 **tablespoons cornstarch**

3 **tablespoons cold water**

1 Spray 4- to 5-quart slow cooker with cooking spray. In slow cooker, mix all ingredients except cornstarch and water.

2 Cover; cook on Low heat setting 8 to 10 hours.

3 In small bowl, mix cornstarch and water until smooth; gradually stir into stew until blended. Increase heat setting to High; cover and cook about 20 minutes longer, stirring occasionally, or until thickened.

1 Serving: Calories 150; Total Fat 0.5g (Saturated Fat 0g, Trans Fat 0g); Cholesterol 0mg; Sodium 550mg; Total Carbohydrate 31g (Dietary Fiber 5g); Protein 4g **Exchanges:** 5 Vegetable **Carbohydrate Choices:** 2

Quick Variation To make this recipe meatless, use vegetable broth in place of chicken broth.

great northern bean and veggie sausage cassoulet

prep time: **20 Minutes** ‖ start to finish: **7 Hours 50 Minutes** ‖ **6 servings (1½ cups each)**

3 medium carrots, sliced (1½ cups)

1 large onion, finely chopped (1 cup)

3 cans (15.5 oz each) great northern beans, drained, rinsed

¾ cup dry white wine or vegetable broth

¼ cup chopped dry-pack sun-dried tomatoes

2 teaspoons dried minced garlic

1 teaspoon dried thyme leaves

1 dried bay leaf

½ teaspoon salt

¼ teaspoon pepper

1 package (14 oz) frozen Italian-style soy-protein sausages with sun-dried tomatoes and basil, each cut into 3 pieces

1 can (14.5 oz) diced tomatoes, undrained

2 tablespoons finely chopped fresh Italian (flat-leaf) parsley

1 tablespoon finely chopped fresh thyme leaves

1 Spray 3- to 4-quart slow cooker with cooking spray. In slow cooker, gently mix carrots, onion, beans, wine, sun-dried tomatoes, garlic, dried thyme, bay leaf, salt and pepper. Arrange soy-protein sausage pieces on top of beans. Pour diced tomatoes over top.

2 Cover; cook on Low heat setting 7½ hours to 8½ hours or 3½ hours to 4½ hours on High heat setting.

3 Just before serving, remove and discard bay leaf. Sprinkle with parsley and fresh thyme.

1 Serving: Calories 580; Total Fat 10g (Saturated Fat 1.5g, Trans Fat 0g); Cholesterol 0mg; Sodium 850mg; Total Carbohydrate 76g (Dietary Fiber 22g); Protein 42g **Exchanges:** 4½ Starch, 2 Vegetable, 3½ Very Lean Meat, 1 Fat **Carbohydrate Choices:** 5

tropical stuffed cabbage rolls

prep time: 30 Minutes || start to finish: 7 Hours 40 Minutes || 4 servings (2 rolls each)

8   large cabbage leaves

1   can (14 oz) reduced-fat (lite) unsweetened coconut milk (not cream of coconut)

½   cup pineapple preserves

1   cup cooked orzo or rosamarina pasta

1   can (15 oz) black beans, drained, rinsed

1   medium onion, chopped (½ cup)

⅓   cup raisins

⅓   cup cashew pieces

2   teaspoons curry powder

½   teaspoon garlic salt

    Flaked coconut, if desired

    Additional cashew pieces, if desired

1 In large bowl, cover cabbage leaves with boiling water. Cover; let stand about 10 minutes or until leaves are limp.

2 Meanwhile, spray 3- to 4-quart slow cooker with cooking spray. In small bowl, mix coconut milk and preserves. Spread ½ cup mixture in bottom of slow cooker; set remaining mixture aside. In medium bowl, mix pasta, beans, onion, raisins, ⅓ cup cashews, curry powder and garlic salt.

3 Remove cabbage leaves from water; drain. Place about ⅓ cup pasta mixture at stem end of each leaf. Roll leaf around pasta mixture, tucking in sides. Place as many cabbage rolls, seam side down, as will comfortably fit in slow cooker. Cover with ⅓ cup of the remaining coconut milk mixture. Repeat with remaining cabbage rolls. Pour remaining coconut milk mixture over rolls.

4 Cover; cook on Low heat setting 7 to 9 hours (or on High heat setting 3 hours 30 minutes to 4 hours 30 minutes).

5 With spatula, carefully remove cabbage rolls, one at a time, from slow cooker; place on serving platter. Sprinkle rolls with coconut and additional cashews.

1 Serving: Calories 670; Total Fat 27g (Saturated Fat 19g, Trans Fat 0g); Cholesterol 0mg; Sodium 620mg; Total Carbohydrate 91g (Dietary Fiber 16g); Protein 16g **Exchanges:** 2 Starch, 3½ Other Carbohydrate, ½ Milk, 1 Vegetable, ½ High-Fat Meat, 3½ Fat **Carbohydrate Choices:** 6

Quick Variation Add even more tropical flavor to this dish by using macadamia nuts in place of the cashews.

red pepper–spinach lasagna

prep time: 30 Minutes ‖ **start to finish:** 5 Hours 30 Minutes ‖ 8 servings

1 jar (26 to 28 oz) tomato pasta sauce

2 medium red bell peppers, chopped

1 medium onion, chopped (½ cup)

2 boxes (9 oz each) frozen chopped spinach, thawed, squeezed to drain

1 can (8 oz) tomato sauce

9 uncooked lasagna noodles

1 jar (16 oz) Alfredo pasta sauce

15 slices (1 oz each) provolone cheese

¼ cup grated Parmesan cheese

1 Spray 5- to 6-quart slow cooker with cooking spray. Spread ¾ cup of the tomato pasta sauce in bottom of slow cooker.

2 In large bowl, mix bell peppers, onion and spinach; stir in remaining tomato pasta sauce and the tomato sauce.

3 Layer 3 lasagna noodles, broken into pieces to fit, over sauce in slow cooker. Top with one-third of the Alfredo sauce, spreading to cover noodles completely. Top with 5 of the cheese slices, overlapping if necessary. Top with one-third of the vegetable mixture (about 2 cups), spreading evenly. Repeat layers twice. Sprinkle Parmesan cheese over top.

4 Cover; cook on Low heat setting 5 to 6 hours.

1 Serving: Calories 630; Total Fat 37g (Saturated Fat 21g, Trans Fat 1g); Cholesterol 95mg; Sodium 1460mg; Total Carbohydrate 48g (Dietary Fiber 5g); Protein 26g **Exchanges:** 1½ Starch, 1½ Low-Fat Milk, 2 Vegetable, ½ Lean Meat, 5½ Fat **Carbohydrate Choices:** 3

time-saver Frozen spinach can be quickly thawed using the microwave. Place frozen blocks of spinach in a 10-inch square microwavable dish. Microwave uncovered on High 3 minutes. Break up blocks; microwave 3 more minutes or until completely thawed. Drain well, squeezing out as much liquid as possible.

CHAPTER
6

soups, stews & chilies

calorie-controlled

coq au vin

prep time: **45 Minutes** || start to finish: **1 Hour 20 Minutes** || **6 servings**

½ cup all-purpose flour

1 teaspoon salt

¼ teaspoon pepper

1 cut-up whole chicken (3 to 3½ lb)

8 slices bacon

¾ cup frozen small whole onions (from 1-lb bag)

1 package (8 oz) sliced fresh mushrooms (about 3 cups)

1 cup chicken broth (from 32-oz carton)

1 cup dry red wine or nonalcoholic red wine

4 medium carrots, cut into 2-inch pieces

1 clove garlic, finely chopped

Bouquet garni*

1 In shallow dish, mix flour, 1 teaspoon of the salt and the pepper. Coat chicken with flour mixture.

2 In 12-inch skillet, cook bacon over medium heat 8 to 10 minutes, turning once, until crisp. Remove bacon with slotted spoon and drain on paper towels; set aside. Cook chicken in bacon drippings over medium heat about 15 minutes, turning occasionally, until browned on all sides.

3 Move chicken to one side of skillet; add onions and mushrooms to other side. Cook uncovered over medium-high heat about 6 minutes, stirring occasionally, until mushrooms are tender. Drain drippings from skillet.

4 Crumble bacon. Stir bacon and remaining ingredients into vegetables. Heat to boiling. Reduce heat; cover and simmer about 35 minutes or until juice of chicken is clear when thickest part is cut to bone (at least 165°F). Remove and discard bouquet garni; skim off excess fat.

1 Serving: Calories 350; Total Fat 19g (Saturated Fat 6g, Trans Fat 0g); Cholesterol 95mg; Sodium 1020mg; Total Carbohydrate 12g (Dietary Fiber 1g); Protein 33g **Exchanges:** 1 Starch, 2 Vegetable, 4 Lean Meat, ½ Fat **Carbohydrate Choices:** 1

* Tie ½ teaspoon dried thyme leaves, 2 large sprigs fresh parsley and 1 dried bay leaf in cheesecloth bag, or place in tea ball.

new potato–chicken stew

prep time: 30 Minutes || **start to finish:** 30 Minutes || **4 servings (1½ cups each)**

2 cups fresh broccoli
   florets or sugar snap
   peas

1 cup water

6 new red potatoes (8 oz),
   cut into fourths

3 boneless skinless chicken
   breasts (12 oz), cut into
   1-inch cubes

1 jar (12 oz) chicken gravy

1 In 3-quart saucepan, mix all ingredients. Heat to boiling, stirring occasionally.

2 Reduce heat; cover and simmer 15 to 20 minutes, stirring occasionally, until potatoes are tender and chicken is no longer pink in center.

1 Serving: Calories 250; Total Fat 8g (Saturated Fat 2g, Trans Fat 0g); Cholesterol 55mg; Sodium 430mg; Total Carbohydrate 22g (Dietary Fiber 3g); Protein 23g **Exchanges:** 1 Starch, 1 Vegetable, 2½ Lean Meat **Carbohydrate Choices:** 1½

chicken, sausage and cabbage stew

prep time: **20 Minutes** || start to finish: **6 Hours 20 Minutes** || **8 servings**

- 2 cups coarsely chopped (1-inch pieces) cabbage
- 1 cup ready-to-eat baby-cut carrots, cut lengthwise into fourths
- 1 cup uncooked wild rice
- 1 medium onion, chopped (½ cup)
- 2 cloves garlic, finely chopped
- 1 package (8 oz) sliced fresh mushrooms (about 3 cups)
- 1 lb boneless skinless chicken thighs, cut into 1½-inch pieces
- 8 oz sweet Italian sausage links (about 2), cut into 1-inch pieces
- 1 carton (32 oz) chicken broth (4 cups)
- 1 can (10¾ oz) condensed cream of mushroom soup

1 Spray 4- to 5-quart slow cooker with cooking spray. In slow cooker, mix all ingredients except broth and soup.

2 In medium bowl, mix broth and soup. Pour over meat and vegetables in slow cooker; stir gently until blended.

3 Cover; cook on Low heat setting 6 to 8 hours.

1 Serving: Calories 310; Total Fat 13g (Saturated Fat 4g, Trans Fat 0g); Cholesterol 55mg; Sodium 830mg; Total Carbohydrate 25g (Dietary Fiber 3g); Protein 24g **Exchanges:** 1 Starch, ½ Other Carbohydrate, 1 Vegetable, 2½ Lean Meat, 1 Fat **Carbohydrate Choices:** 1½

white chicken chili

prep time: **15 Minutes** || start to finish: **40 Minutes** || **6 servings (1⅓ cups each)**

1 tablespoon vegetable oil

1 large onion, chopped (1 cup)

2 cloves garlic, finely chopped

3 cups chicken broth (from 32-oz carton)

1 can (11 oz) vacuum-packed white shoepeg or whole kernel sweet corn, drained

1 can (15.5 oz) great northern beans, drained

1 can (15.5 oz) butter beans, drained

2 tablespoons chopped fresh cilantro

2 tablespoons lime juice

1 teaspoon ground cumin

½ teaspoon dried oregano leaves

¼ teaspoon red pepper sauce

¼ teaspoon salt

2 cups chopped cooked chicken breast

1 In 4-quart Dutch oven or stockpot, heat oil over medium heat. Add onion and garlic; cook 4 to 6 minutes, stirring occasionally, until onion is tender.

2 Stir in all remaining ingredients except chicken. Heat to boiling. Reduce heat; simmer uncovered 20 minutes.

3 Stir in chicken. Simmer about 5 minutes longer or until hot.

1 Serving: Calories 360; Total Fat 6g (Saturated Fat 1.5g, Trans Fat 0g); Cholesterol 40mg; Sodium 920mg; Total Carbohydrate 46g (Dietary Fiber 11g); Protein 31g **Exchanges:** 2 Starch, 3 Vegetable, 2 Lean Meat **Carbohydrate Choices:** 3

chicken-tortilla soup

prep time: **35 Minutes** ‖ start to finish: **35 Minutes** ‖ **6 servings (1 cup each)**

 1 **carton (32 oz) chicken broth**
 1 **cup chunky-style salsa**
 2 **cups shredded deli rotisserie chicken (from 2- to 2½-lb chicken)**
 ¾ **cup crushed tortilla chips**
 1 **medium avocado, pitted, peeled and chopped**
1½ **cups shredded Monterey Jack cheese (6 oz)**
 2 **tablespoons chopped fresh cilantro**
    Lime wedges, if desired

1 In 3-quart saucepan, heat broth, salsa and chicken to boiling over medium-high heat, stirring occasionally.

2 Meanwhile, divide crushed chips among 6 individual serving bowls.

3 Spoon hot soup over chips. Top with avocado, cheese and cilantro. Serve with lime wedges.

1 Serving: Calories 330; Total Fat 20g (Saturated Fat 8g, Trans Fat 0g); Cholesterol 65mg; Sodium 1390mg; Total Carbohydrate 13g (Dietary Fiber 2g); Protein 24g **Exchanges:** 1 Starch, 3 Lean Meat, 2 Fat **Carbohydrate Choices:** 1

time-saver When you pick up the rotisserie chicken for this recipe, get an extra chicken. It's easy to keep shredding chicken when you can do a bunch all at once. Then freeze what you're not using now for another meal or two.

southwestern turkey soup

prep time: **30 Minutes** ‖ start to finish: **30 Minutes** ‖ **6 servings (about 1⅓ cups each)**

1 tablespoon vegetable oil

2 medium green bell peppers, cut into 1-inch pieces

2 cups cubed, peeled, cooked butternut squash

2 cups shredded cooked turkey or chicken

2 cups chicken broth (from 32-oz carton)

1 can (16 oz) refried black beans

1 can (14 oz) diced tomatoes, undrained

1 package (1 oz) 40% less-sodium taco seasoning mix

1 Heat oil in Dutch oven or large saucepan over medium heat; add bell peppers. Cook 6 to 10 minutes, stirring occasionally, until peppers are almost crisp-tender. Stir in remaining ingredients.

2 Heat to boiling over medium heat, stirring frequently to prevent sticking to bottom of pan. Reduce heat; simmer uncovered 10 minutes, stirring occasionally, to blend flavors.

1 Serving: Calories 250; Total Fat 8g (Saturated Fat 2g, Trans Fat 0g); Cholesterol 35mg; Sodium 1150mg; Total Carbohydrate 26g (Dietary Fiber 7g); Protein 18g **Exchanges:** 1½ Starch, ½ Vegetable, 2 Lean Meat **Carbohydrate Choices:** 2

time-savers Cut-up, ready-to-cook squash can be found in the produce section of many grocery stores and club stores during the fall and winter.

Also, if you are using leftover cooked squash that's already mashed, simply stir it in with other ingredients for a thicker soup.

turkey-spaetzle soup

prep time: 25 Minutes ‖ **start to finish:** 25 Minutes ‖ 6 servings

2 tablespoons vegetable oil

1 large onion, finely chopped (1 cup)

1 medium carrot, finely chopped (½ cup)

1 medium stalk celery, finely chopped (½ cup)

1 clove garlic, finely chopped

¼ cup all-purpose flour

1 tablespoon chopped fresh or 2 teaspoons dried thyme leaves

¼ teaspoon pepper

2 cups diced cooked turkey

6 cups chicken broth (from two 32-oz cartons)

1 bag (12 oz) frozen spaetzle

Chopped fresh parsley, if desired

1 In 4-quart saucepan, heat oil over medium-high heat. Add onion, carrot, celery and garlic; cook about 2 minutes, stirring frequently, until crisp-tender.

2 Gradually stir in flour, thyme and pepper; cook and stir about 1 minute. Stir in turkey and broth; heat to boiling.

3 Stir in frozen spaetzle. Cook 2 to 3 minutes, stirring occasionally, until spaetzle are tender. Sprinkle with parsley.

1 Serving: Calories 240; Total Fat 10g (Saturated Fat 2.5g, Trans Fat 0g); Cholesterol 70mg; Sodium 1180mg; Total Carbohydrate 17g (Dietary Fiber 2g); Protein 21g **Exchanges:** 1 Starch, 2½ Lean Meat, ½ Fat **Carbohydrate Choices:** 1

Quick Variation If you prefer, substitute 3 cups frozen egg noodles (from 1-pound bag) for the spaetzle.

seasoned tomato-beef stew

prep time: 15 Minutes ‖ **start to finish:** 3 Hours 45 Minutes ‖ 8 servings

1 lb beef stew meat, cut into ½-inch pieces

1 medium onion, cut into 8 wedges

1 bag (8 oz) ready-to-eat baby-cut carrots (about 30)

1 can (14.5 oz) diced tomatoes, undrained

1 can (10½ oz) condensed beef broth

1 can (8 oz) tomato sauce

⅓ cup all-purpose flour

1 tablespoon Worcestershire sauce

1 teaspoon salt

1 teaspoon sugar

1 teaspoon dried marjoram leaves

¼ teaspoon pepper

12 small red potatoes (1½ lb), cut into fourths

2 cups sliced fresh mushrooms (about 5 oz) or 1 package (about 3½ oz) fresh shiitake mushrooms, sliced

1 Heat oven to 325°F. In 4-quart ovenproof Dutch oven, mix all ingredients except potatoes and mushrooms. Cover; bake 2 hours, stirring once.

2 Stir in potatoes and mushrooms. Cover; bake 1 hour to 1 hour 30 minutes longer or until beef and vegetables are tender.

1 Serving: Calories 310; Total Fat 7g (Saturated Fat 2.5g, Trans Fat 0g); Cholesterol 35mg; Sodium 820mg; Total Carbohydrate 43g (Dietary Fiber 6g); Protein 18g **Exchanges:** 2 Starch, 2 Vegetable, 1 Medium-Fat Meat, ½ Fat **Carbohydrate Choices:** 3

Quick Variation For variety, add 1 cup diced bell pepper (any color) with the onion; omit the mushrooms. Substitute 1 additional can (14.5 ounces) diced tomatoes for the tomato sauce.

beef and bean chili

prep time: 25 Minutes ‖ **start to finish:** 8 Hours 25 Minutes ‖ 8 servings (1 cup each)

1 tablespoon olive or vegetable oil

1 large onion, coarsely chopped (1 cup)

2 teaspoons finely chopped garlic

2 tablespoons chili powder

1 tablespoon ground cumin

1 teaspoon salt

⅛ teaspoon pepper

2 lb beef stew meat

2 cans (15 oz each) black beans, drained, rinsed

2 cans (14.5 oz each) diced tomatoes with green chiles, undrained

½ cup water

1 In 12-inch skillet, heat oil over medium-high heat. Add onion and garlic; cook 4 to 5 minutes, stirring frequently, until onion is softened.

2 Stir in chili powder, cumin, salt, pepper and beef. Cook 6 to 8 minutes, stirring occasionally, until beef is lightly browned.

3 Spray 3- to 4-quart slow cooker with cooking spray. Place beef mixture in slow cooker. Stir in beans, tomatoes and water.

4 Cover; cook on Low heat setting 8 to 10 hours. Stir well before serving.

1 Serving: Calories 370; Total Fat 7g (Saturated Fat 2g, Trans Fat 0g); Cholesterol 75mg; Sodium 650mg; Total Carbohydrate 36g (Dietary Fiber 14g); Protein 41g **Exchanges:** 2 Starch, 1 Vegetable, 4½ Very Lean Meat, ½ Fat **Carbohydrate Choices:** 2½

Quick Variation If you're not a fan of black beans, kidney beans are a great substitute in this chili.

skillet nacho chili

prep time: 30 Minutes ‖ start to finish: 30 Minutes ‖ 4 servings

1 lb lean (at least 80%) ground beef

1 medium onion, chopped (½ cup)

1 can (19 oz) hearty tomato soup

1 can (15 to 16 oz) spicy chili beans in sauce, undrained

1 can (4.5 oz) chopped green chiles, undrained

1 cup frozen corn

1 cup shredded Cheddar cheese (4 oz)

2 cups corn chips

1 Spray 12-inch skillet with cooking spray; heat over medium-high heat. Cook beef and onion in skillet 5 to 7 minutes, stirring frequently, until beef is browned and onion is tender; drain.

2 Stir soup, chili beans, green chiles and corn into beef mixture. Heat to boiling; reduce heat to medium. Cook 8 to 10 minutes, stirring occasionally, until sauce is slightly thickened and corn is cooked.

3 Sprinkle each serving with cheese. Serve with corn chips.

1 Serving: Calories 590; Total Fat 28g (Saturated Fat 12g, Trans Fat 1g); Cholesterol 100mg; Sodium 2160mg; Total Carbohydrate 48g (Dietary Fiber 8g); Protein 35g **Exchanges:** 2 Starch, 1 Other Carbohydrate, 4 Medium-Fat Meat, 1½ Fat **Carbohydrate Choices:** 3

Quick Variation Ground turkey can be used in place of the ground beef in this recipe.

easy vegetable-beef soup

prep time: 35 Minutes ‖ **start to finish:** 35 Minutes ‖ **6 servings (1½ cups each)**

1 lb ground beef sirloin

1 cup chopped onion (1 large)

4½ teaspoons finely chopped garlic

1 teaspoon dried Italian seasoning

½ teaspoon pepper

¼ teaspoon salt

SOUP

2½ cups water

1 bag (16 oz) frozen mixed vegetables

1 can (14.5 oz) Italian-style stewed tomatoes, undrained, chopped

1 can (8 oz) tomato sauce

1 In 5-quart Dutch oven or saucepan, cook beef, onion, garlic, Italian seasoning, pepper, and salt over medium-high heat 5 to 7 minutes, stirring occasionally, until beef is thoroughly cooked; drain.

2 Stir in remaining ingredients. Heat to boiling over medium-high heat. Reduce heat; cover and simmer 20 minutes, stirring occasionally, until hot.

1 Serving: Calories 210; Total Fat 9g (Saturated Fat 3.5g, Trans Fat 0.5g); Cholesterol 45mg; Sodium 730mg; Total Carbohydrate 16g (Dietary Fiber 4g); Protein 16g **Exchanges:** ½ Other Carbohydrate, 1 Vegetable, 2 Medium-Fat Meat **Carbohydrate Choices:** 1

bratwurst and vegetable soup

prep time: 35 Minutes || **start to finish:** 35 Minutes || 5 servings (1⅓ cups each)

1 teaspoon caraway seed

1 medium baking potato, peeled, cut into ½-inch pieces (1 cup)

1 cup ready-to-eat baby-cut carrots

¾ cup fresh green beans (about 4 oz), cut into 1-inch pieces

¼ cup chopped fresh parsley

¼ teaspoon pepper

2 cups reduced-sodium beef broth

4 smoked beef bratwurst (from 12-oz package), cut into ½-inch-thick slices (about 1½ cups)

1 can (15.5 oz) great northern beans, drained, rinsed

1 can (14.5 oz) diced tomatoes with garlic and onion, undrained

1 In 3-quart saucepan, cook and stir caraway seed 1 to 2 minutes over medium heat or until toasted.

2 Stir in remaining ingredients. Increase heat to high; heat to boiling. Reduce heat; cover and simmer 15 to 20 minutes, stirring occasionally, until vegetables are tender.

1 Serving: Calories 320; Total Fat 13g (Saturated Fat 5g, Trans Fat 0g); Cholesterol 20mg; Sodium 1560mg; Total Carbohydrate 33g (Dietary Fiber 8g); Protein 16g **Exchanges:** 2 Starch, 1 Vegetable, 1 Medium-Fat Meat, 1½ Fat **Carbohydrate Choices:** 2

lentil and bratwurst stew

prep time: **35 Minutes** ‖ start to finish: **2 Hours 15 Minutes** ‖ **6 servings (1⅓ cups each)**

3   **fresh bratwurst links**

3   **cups water**

1   **large leek, cut in half lengthwise, then crosswise into ½-inch pieces (3 cups)**

1   **medium stalk celery, sliced (½ cup)**

1   **medium carrot, sliced (½ cup)**

1   **cup dried green lentils, sorted, rinsed**

½   **teaspoon salt**

1   **cup Chianti or dry red wine**

1   **can (14.5 oz) diced tomatoes, undrained**

2   **cups fresh baby spinach leaves**

1 In 3-quart saucepan, cook bratwurst over medium heat until browned on all sides.

2 Carefully pour in 1 cup of the water. Heat to boiling. Reduce heat; cover and simmer 6 to 8 minutes, turning bratwurst occasionally, until no longer pink in center. Remove bratwurst from saucepan; cover and refrigerate. Discard cooking liquid.

3 Into same saucepan, pour remaining 2 cups water. Stir in all remaining ingredients except bratwurst and spinach. Heat to boiling. Reduce heat; cover and simmer 1 hour 15 minutes to 1 hour 30 minutes or until lentils are tender.

4 Cut bratwurst into ½-inch slices; stir into stew. Cook about 3 minutes or until bratwurst is hot. Stir in spinach. Cook uncovered 1 to 2 minutes longer or just until spinach is wilted.

1 Serving: Calories 300; Total Fat 12g (Saturated Fat 4.5g, Trans Fat 0g); Cholesterol 25mg; Sodium 780mg; Total Carbohydrate 31g (Dietary Fiber 7g); Protein 14g **Exchanges:** 1½ Starch, 2 Vegetable, 1 Very Lean Meat, 2 Fat **Carbohydrate Choices:** 2

healthy twist Reduce fat and calories from this dish by substituting fully cooked chicken sausage (any flavor) for the bratwurst. There's no need to cook it first. Simply slice it and add it to the stew in step 3 and continue as directed in recipe.

Heirloom Recipe and New Twist

down-home pork stew

prep time: 1 Hour || **start to finish:** 1 Hour || 6 servings

1 lb boneless pork shoulder, cut into ¾-inch cubes

¼ cup all-purpose flour

½ teaspoon peppered seasoned salt

1 tablespoon vegetable oil

2 medium dark-orange sweet potatoes, peeled, cut into ¾-inch cubes (about 3 cups)

2 cups frozen whole kernel corn

2 cups frozen chopped collard greens (from 1-lb bag)

1 can (15 to 16 oz) black-eyed peas, drained, rinsed

1 can (14 oz) roasted garlic–seasoned chicken broth

2 tablespoons Worcestershire sauce

½ teaspoon dried thyme leaves

⅛ teaspoon ground red pepper (cayenne)

1 In large bowl, mix pork, flour and seasoned salt until pork is coated. In 12-inch nonstick skillet, heat oil over medium-high heat. Add pork; cook 8 to 10 minutes, stirring occasionally, until browned.

2 Add remaining ingredients to pork in skillet. Heat to boiling. Reduce heat to low; cover and simmer 30 to 40 minutes, stirring occasionally, until pork is tender.

1 Serving: Calories 400; Total Fat 13g (Saturated Fat 4g, Trans Fat 0g); Cholesterol 50mg; Sodium 680mg; Total Carbohydrate 44g (Dietary Fiber 7g); Protein 27g **Exchanges:** 3 Starch, 2½ Lean Meat, ½ Fat **Carbohydrate Choices:** 3

Quick Variation Plain chicken broth can be used, but increase the seasonings by adding 1 or 2 cloves finely chopped garlic.

pumpkin-pork stew

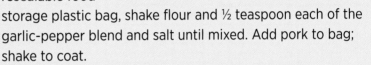

calorie-controlled

prep time: 1 Hour ‖ **start to finish:** 1 Hour 25 Minutes ‖ 6 servings (1⅓ cups each)

¼ cup all-purpose flour

1 teaspoon garlic-pepper blend

1 teaspoon salt

4 boneless pork sirloin chops, ½ inch thick (1½ lb), cut into 1-inch pieces

3 tablespoons vegetable oil

1 can (15 oz) pumpkin (not pumpkin pie mix)

2½ cups chicken broth (from 32-oz carton)

1 tablespoon finely chopped chipotle chiles in adobo sauce (from 7-oz can)

1 teaspoon dried oregano leaves

1 dried bay leaf

2 cups cubed (1-inch) peeled butternut or buttercup squash (about 12 oz)

2 cups frozen cut green beans (from 12-oz bag)

1 medium red bell pepper, cut into 1-inch pieces (1¼ cups)

1 In 1-gallon resealable food-storage plastic bag, shake flour and ½ teaspoon each of the garlic-pepper blend and salt until mixed. Add pork to bag; shake to coat.

2 In 5-quart Dutch oven or stockpot, heat oil over medium-high heat. Add coated pork; cook, stirring occasionally, until pork is white with golden brown edges. Discard any remaining flour mixture.

3 Stir in pumpkin, broth, chiles in adobo, oregano, bay leaf and remaining ½ teaspoon each garlic-pepper blend and salt. Heat to boiling, scraping browned bits off bottom of Dutch oven. Reduce heat to low; cover and simmer 30 minutes, scraping bottom of Dutch oven occasionally to prevent sticking.

4 Stir in squash and green beans. Heat to boiling. Reduce heat; cover and simmer 15 minutes. Stir in bell pepper. Cover; simmer 5 to 7 minutes longer or until bell pepper is crisp-tender. Remove and discard bay leaf before serving.

1 Serving: Calories 320; Total Fat 15g (Saturated Fat 4g, Trans Fat 0g); Cholesterol 65mg; Sodium 880mg; Total Carbohydrate 18g (Dietary Fiber 5g); Protein 27g **Exchanges:** 1 Starch, 1 Vegetable, 3 Lean Meat, 1 Fat **Carbohydrate Choices:** 1

spicy thai pork stew

prep time: 30 Minutes ‖ **start to finish:** 1 Hour 40 Minutes ‖ 6 servings (1 cup each)

⅓ cup all-purpose flour

½ teaspoon garlic-pepper blend

4 boneless pork loin chops, 1 inch thick (1½ lb), cut into 1-inch cubes

3 tablespoons vegetable oil

1 bottle (11.5 oz) peanut sauce

1 cup chicken broth (from 32-oz carton)

1 teaspoon crushed red pepper flakes

2 cups cubed (1-inch) peeled butternut squash (about 12 oz)

1 medium red bell pepper, cut into 1-inch pieces (1¼ cups)

4 oz fresh snow pea pods (1 cup), strings removed, cut diagonally in half

Hot cooked white rice, if desired

1 In 1-gallon resealable food-storage plastic bag, shake flour and garlic-pepper blend to mix. Add pork; seal bag and shake to coat.

2 In 5-quart Dutch oven or stockpot, heat oil over medium heat. Add coated pork; cook, stirring occasionally, until pork is evenly golden brown. Stir in peanut sauce, broth and red pepper. Heat to boiling. Boil 1 minute, scraping browned bits off bottom of Dutch oven. Reduce heat to low; cover and simmer 30 minutes.

3 Add squash. Cover; simmer 30 minutes or until pork and squash are tender.

4 Stir in bell pepper and snow pea pods. Simmer uncovered 5 to 7 minutes or until bell pepper is crisp-tender. Serve over hot cooked white rice.

1 Serving: Calories 480; Total Fat 30g (Saturated Fat 7g, Trans Fat 0g); Cholesterol 70mg; Sodium 350mg; Total Carbohydrate 19g (Dietary Fiber 3g); Protein 34g **Exchanges:** 1 Starch, ½ Vegetable, 4 Lean Meat, 3½ Fat **Carbohydrate Choices:** 1

zesty autumn pork stew

prep time: 25 Minutes ‖ **start to finish:** 25 Minutes ‖ **4 servings**

1 **lb pork tenderloin, cut into 1-inch cubes**

2 **medium dark-orange sweet potatoes, peeled, cubed (2 cups)**

1 **medium green bell pepper, chopped (1 cup)**

2 **cloves garlic, finely chopped**

1 **cup coleslaw mix (shredded cabbage and carrots)**

1 **teaspoon Cajun seasoning**

1 **can (14 oz) chicken broth**

1 Spray 4-quart stockpot with cooking spray; heat over medium-high heat. Cook pork in Dutch oven, stirring occasionally, until browned.

2 Stir in remaining ingredients. Heat to boiling; reduce heat. Cover; simmer about 15 minutes, stirring once, until sweet potatoes are tender.

1 Serving: Calories 240; Total Fat 5g (Saturated Fat 1.5g, Trans Fat 0g); Cholesterol 70mg; Sodium 640mg; Total Carbohydrate 18g (Dietary Fiber 3g); Protein 30g **Exchanges:** 1 Starch, 4 Very Lean Meat, ½ Fat **Carbohydrate Choices:** 1

Quick Variation Canned vacuum-packed sweet potatoes, cubed, can be substituted for the fresh sweet potatoes. Add them after you reduce the heat in step 2, and remember to stir the mixture gently, because canned sweet potatoes are very soft and tender.

minestrone with italian sausage

prep time: 45 Minutes || start to finish: 45 Minutes || 7 servings (1½ cups each)

1 tablespoon olive or vegetable oil

1 lb bulk sweet Italian pork sausage

2 medium carrots, coarsely chopped (1 cup)

1 medium onion, chopped (½ cup)

2 teaspoons dried basil leaves

2 teaspoons finely chopped garlic

5¼ cups beef broth (from two 32-oz cartons)

1 can (14.5 oz) diced tomatoes, undrained

1 can (15.5 oz) great northern beans, drained, rinsed

1 cup uncooked small elbow macaroni (4 oz)

1 medium zucchini, cut in half lengthwise, then crosswise into ¼-inch slices (1 cup)

1 cup frozen cut green beans

1 In 5-quart Dutch oven or stockpot, heat oil over medium-high heat. Add sausage, carrots, onion, basil and garlic; cook 5 to 7 minutes, stirring frequently, until sausage is no longer pink. Drain.

2 Stir broth, tomatoes and great northern beans into sausage mixture. Heat to boiling. Reduce heat to medium-low; cover and cook 7 to 8 minutes, stirring occasionally.

3 Stir in macaroni, zucchini and frozen green beans. Heat to boiling. Cook over medium-high heat 5 to 6 minutes, stirring occasionally, until vegetables are hot and macaroni is tender.

1 Serving: Calories 380; Total Fat 16g (Saturated Fat 5g, Trans Fat 0g); Cholesterol 25mg; Sodium 1400mg; Total Carbohydrate 38g (Dietary Fiber 6g); Protein 20g **Exchanges:** 2 Starch, 1 Vegetable, 1½ Medium-Fat Meat, 1½ Fat **Carbohydrate Choices:** 2½

Quick Variation Substitute 1 can (15.5 ounces) great northern beans or your favorite canned beans for the sausage and use vegetable broth instead of beef broth.

cuban black bean soup

prep time: **35 Minutes** || start to finish: **2 Hours 35 Minutes** || **8 servings (1½ cups each)**

2 tablespoons vegetable oil

1 cup chopped onion (1 large)

3 cloves garlic, finely chopped

1 bag (16 oz) dried black beans, sorted, rinsed (2 cups)

1 cup finely chopped cooked ham

3 cups beef broth (from 32-oz carton)

3 cups water

¼ cup dark rum or apple cider

1½ teaspoons ground cumin

1½ teaspoons dried oregano leaves

1 medium green bell pepper, chopped (1 cup)

1 large tomato, chopped (1 cup)

Chopped hard-cooked eggs, if desired

Additional chopped onion, if desired

1 In 4-quart Dutch oven or saucepan, heat oil over medium heat. Add 1 cup onion and the garlic; cook 4 to 6 minutes, stirring occasionally, until onion is tender.

2 Stir in all remaining ingredients except eggs and additional onion. Heat to boiling. Boil 2 minutes. Reduce heat; cover and simmer about 2 hours or until beans are tender. Serve soup topped with eggs and onion.

1 Serving: Calories 290; Total Fat 6g (Saturated Fat 1g, Trans Fat 0g); Cholesterol 10mg; Sodium 610mg; Total Carbohydrate 40g (Dietary Fiber 14g); Protein 19g **Exchanges:** 2 Starch, 2 Vegetable, 1 Very Lean Meat **Carbohydrate Choices:** 2½

two-potato ham chowder

prep time: **30 Minutes** || start to finish: **30 Minutes** || **5 servings (1¼ cups each)**

½ cup chopped leek or onion

2 cups reduced-sodium chicken broth (from 32-oz carton)

2 medium baking potatoes, peeled, each cut into 6 pieces

2 cups cubed (½-inch) peeled dark-orange sweet potatoes (about 2 medium)

1 cup diced cooked ham (from 8-oz package)

1 cup frozen sweet peas (from 12-oz bag)

2 tablespoons chopped fresh chives

½ teaspoon salt

¼ teaspoon pepper

1 cup half-and-half or milk

1 Spray 3-quart saucepan with cooking spray; heat over medium heat. Add leek; cook and stir about 3 minutes or until softened. Increase heat to high. Add broth and baking potatoes. Heat to boiling. Reduce heat; cover and gently simmer 5 minutes.

2 Add sweet potatoes. Cover; gently simmer about 10 minutes or until potatoes are tender when pierced with fork.

3 Using slotted spoon, remove baking potatoes from saucepan; place in blender. With lid on saucepan, carefully drain off broth into blender, leaving leek and sweet potatoes in saucepan. Cover blender; puree potato mixture until smooth. Return mixture to saucepan.

4 Stir in remaining ingredients. Cook over medium heat about 8 minutes, stirring occasionally, until thoroughly heated.

1 Serving: Calories 240; Total Fat 8g (Saturated Fat 4.5g, Trans Fat 0g); Cholesterol 35mg; Sodium 900mg; Total Carbohydrate 28g (Dietary Fiber 4g); Protein 12g **Exchanges:** 1½ Starch, 1 Vegetable, ½ Very Lean Meat, ½ Lean Meat, 1 Fat **Carbohydrate Choices:** 2

time-saver This is a great soup to take to work for lunch. Pour leftovers into microwavable containers. Cool slightly; cover and refrigerate.

hearty seafood stew

prep time: 50 Minutes ‖ **start to finish:** 1 Hour ‖ 6 servings

- 2 tablespoons vegetable oil
- 2 medium carrots, thinly sliced (1 cup)
- 2 medium stalks celery, sliced (1 cup)
- 1 large onion, chopped (1 cup)
- 1 clove garlic, finely chopped
- 1 can (14.5 oz) stewed tomatoes, undrained
- 2 cups water
- 1 medium potato, cut into ½-inch pieces
- 1 tablespoon beef bouillon granules
- 1 lb cod or other medium-firm fish fillets, cut into 1-inch pieces
- 8 oz uncooked medium shrimp, thawed if frozen, peeled, deveined
- 1 can (15.5 oz) great northern beans, drained, rinsed
- 1 small zucchini, cut in half lengthwise, then crosswise into slices
- 1 teaspoon chopped fresh or ¼ teaspoon dried thyme leaves
- ½ teaspoon pepper

1 In 4-quart Dutch oven, heat oil over medium-high heat. Add carrots, celery, onion and garlic; cook about 5 minutes, stirring frequently, until vegetables are tender.

2 Stir in tomatoes, water, potato, and bouillon. Heat to boiling. Reduce heat; cover and simmer 20 minutes, stirring occasionally.

3 Stir in cod, shrimp, beans, zucchini, thyme and pepper. Heat to boiling. Reduce heat; cover and simmer 6 to 10 minutes or until fish flakes easily with fork and shrimp are pink. Serve topped with parsley if desired.

1 Serving: Calories 290; Total Fat 6g (Saturated Fat 1g, Trans Fat 0g); Cholesterol 75mg; Sodium 740mg; Total Carbohydrate 32g (Dietary Fiber 7g); Protein 26g **Exchanges:** 2 Starch, 1 Vegetable, 2½ Very Lean Meat, ½ Fat **Carbohydrate Choices:** 2

fish and vegetable soup

prep time: **25 Minutes** || start to finish: **35 Minutes** || **4 servings (1½ cups each)**

1 tablespoon butter

¼ cup chopped onion

1 clove garlic, finely chopped

3½ cups chicken broth (from 32-oz carton)

1 cup thinly sliced carrots

1 cup frozen cut green beans

½ cup frozen whole kernel corn

½ teaspoon salt

½ teaspoon dried basil leaves

¼ teaspoon dried oregano leaves

⅛ teaspoon pepper

1 lb firm white fish fillets (such as cod, haddock, halibut or orange roughy), cut into 1-inch cubes

1 In 3-quart saucepan or Dutch oven, melt butter over medium heat. Add onion and garlic; cook and stir 2 to 3 minutes or just until garlic begins to brown.

2 Stir in all remaining ingredients except fish. Heat to boiling. Reduce heat; cover and simmer 8 minutes.

3 Add fish; cook uncovered 5 to 7 minutes, stirring occasionally, until fish flakes easily with fork and vegetables are tender.

1 Serving: Calories 190; Total Fat 4.5g (Saturated Fat 2g, Trans Fat 0g); Cholesterol 70mg; Sodium 1170mg; Total Carbohydrate 11g (Dietary Fiber 2g); Protein 25g **Exchanges:** ½ Starch, 1 Vegetable, 3 Very Lean Meat, ½ Fat **Carbohydrate Choices:** 1

new england clam chowder

prep time: 15 Minutes ‖ **start to finish:** 30 Minutes ‖ 4 servings (1¼ cups each)

4 slices bacon, cut into ½-inch pieces

1 medium onion, chopped (½ cup)

1 medium stalk celery, sliced (½ cup)

2 cans (6½ oz each) minced or chopped clams, drained, ¼ cup liquid reserved

2¾ cups milk or half-and-half

2 medium potatoes, peeled, diced (2 cups)

¼ teaspoon salt

Dash pepper

¼ cup all-purpose flour

Chopped fresh parsley, if desired

1 In 3-quart saucepan, cook bacon, onion and celery over medium heat, stirring occasionally, until bacon is crisp and onion is tender; drain.

2 Stir clams, reserved clam liquid, ¾ cup of the milk, the potatoes, salt and pepper into bacon and onion. Heat to boiling. Reduce heat; cover and simmer about 15 minutes or until potatoes are tender.

3 In medium bowl, beat remaining 2 cups milk and the flour with whisk until smooth and blended. Stir into clam mixture. Heat to boiling, stirring frequently. Boil and stir 1 minute or until thickened. Sprinkle each serving with parsley.

1 Serving: Calories 240; Total Fat 5g (Saturated Fat 1.5g, Trans Fat 0g); Cholesterol 75mg; Sodium 490mg; Total Carbohydrate 19g (Dietary Fiber 1g); Protein 29g **Exchanges:** ½ Starch, ½ Low-Fat Milk, 1 Vegetable, 3 Very Lean Meat, 1 Fat **Carbohydrate Choices:** 1

Quick Variation If desired, substitute 1 pint shucked fresh clams with their liquid for the canned clams. Chop the clams and stir in with the potato in step 2.

apple, cinnamon and butternut squash soup

prep time: 25 Minutes || start to finish: 45 Minutes || 8 servings (1 cup each)

8 cups cubed, seeded and peeled butternut squash (2 medium)

1 large apple, peeled, chopped

1 large onion, cut into 1-inch pieces

2 tablespoons packed brown sugar

¾ teaspoon salt

¾ teaspoon ground cinnamon

⅛ teaspoon pepper

3 cups chicken broth (from 32-oz carton)

¾ cup milk

1 container (6 oz) Greek fat-free plain yogurt

2 tablespoons chopped fresh chives

1 In Dutch oven or stockpot, mix squash, apple, onion, brown sugar, salt, cinnamon and pepper. Add broth. Cover; heat to boiling over medium-high heat. Reduce heat; simmer about 20 minutes or until squash is tender.

2 In blender or food processor, place one-third of mixture. Cover and blend until smooth; return to Dutch oven. Repeat twice to blend remaining soup.

3 Stir in milk and yogurt. Heat over low heat, stirring occasionally, just until thoroughly heated. Serve soup topped with chives.

1 Serving: Calories 130; Total Fat 0.5g (Saturated Fat 0g, Trans Fat 0g); Cholesterol 0mg; Sodium 570mg; Total Carbohydrate 25g (Dietary Fiber 2g); Protein 4g **Exchanges:** ½ Starch, 1 Other Carbohydrate, 1 Vegetable **Carbohydrate Choices:** 1½

time-saver Purchase already peeled and cut-up squash if available at your grocery store. Or, you can use a swivel-headed peeler and make quick work of peeling the squash.

Quick Variation To make this recipe meatless, use vegetable broth in place of chicken broth.

wild rice soup

prep time: **30 Minutes** ‖ start to finish: **30 Minutes** ‖ **4 servings (1¼ cups each)**

2 tablespoons butter

2 medium stalks celery, sliced (1 cup)

1 medium carrot, coarsely shredded (1 cup)

1 medium onion, chopped (½ cup)

1 small green bell pepper, chopped (½ cup)

¼ cup Original Bisquick or Bisquick Heart Smart mix

½ teaspoon salt

¼ teaspoon pepper

¼ teaspoon dried thyme leaves, if desired

1 cup water

1 can (10½ oz) condensed chicken broth

1½ cups canned or frozen cooked wild rice

1 cup half-and-half

⅓ cup slivered almonds, toasted*

¼ cup chopped fresh parsley

1 In 3-quart saucepan, melt butter over medium-high heat. Add celery, carrot, onion and bell pepper; cook about 4 minutes, stirring occasionally, until tender.

2 Stir in Bisquick mix, salt, pepper and thyme. Stir in water, broth and wild rice. Heat to boiling, stirring frequently. Reduce heat to low; cover and simmer 15 minutes, stirring occasionally.

3 Stir in half-and-half, almonds and parsley. Heat just until hot (do not boil).

1 Serving: Calories 320; Total Fat 19g (Saturated Fat 9g, Trans Fat 1g); Cholesterol 40mg; Sodium 1150mg; Total Carbohydrate 26g (Dietary Fiber 4g); Protein 10g **Exchanges:** 1½ Starch, 1 Vegetable, ½ High-Fat Meat, 3 Fat **Carbohydrate Choices:** 2

* To toast almonds, spread in shallow pan. Bake at 350°F for 6 to 10 minutes stirring occasionally until light brown.

healthy twist To cut down on fat and calories, spray the saucepan with cooking spray before heating and omit the butter. Use Bisquick Heart Smart mix, substitute 1 cup evaporated fat-free milk for the half-and-half and decrease almonds to 3 tablespoons.

lentil-vegetable soup

prep time: 10 Minutes ‖ **start to finish:** 50 Minutes ‖ 6 servings

1   large onion, chopped
    (1 cup)

2   teaspoons chili powder

1   teaspoon salt

1   teaspoon ground cumin

2   cloves garlic, finely
    chopped

1   can (6 oz) spicy tomato
    juice

3   cups water

1   cup (8 oz) dried lentils,
    sorted, rinsed

2   cups diced tomatoes
    (from 28-oz can),
    undrained

1   can (4.5 oz) chopped
    green chiles, undrained

1   cup fresh or frozen whole
    kernel corn

2   small zucchini, cut into
    julienne strips (2 cups)

1 In 3-quart saucepan, heat onion, chili powder, salt, cumin, garlic and tomato juice to boiling. Reduce heat; cover and simmer 5 minutes.

2 Stir in water, lentils, tomatoes and chiles. Heat to boiling. Reduce heat; cover and simmer 20 minutes.

3 Stir in corn. Cover; simmer 10 minutes. Stir in zucchini. Cover; simmer about 5 minutes longer or until lentils and zucchini are tender.

1 Serving: Calories 190; Total Fat 1g (Saturated Fat 0g, Trans Fat 0g); Cholesterol 0mg; Sodium 790mg; Total Carbohydrate 34g (Dietary Fiber 8g); Protein 10g **Exchanges:** 2 Starch, ½ Very Lean Meat **Carbohydrate Choices:** 2

italian bean soup with greens

prep time: 20 Minutes || **start to finish:** 1 Hour 10 Minutes || 8 servings (1⅓ cups each)

2 tablespoons olive oil

2 medium carrots, sliced (1 cup)

1 large onion, chopped (1 cup)

1 medium stalk celery, chopped (⅓ cup)

2 cloves garlic, finely chopped

2 cans (15 to 15.5 oz each) great northern or cannellini beans, drained, rinsed

1 can (28 oz) diced tomatoes, undrained

2 teaspoons dried basil leaves

1 teaspoon dried oregano leaves

½ teaspoon salt

¼ teaspoon pepper

1 carton (32 oz) vegetable broth (4 cups)

4 cups packed fresh spinach leaves

½ cup shredded Parmesan cheese (2 oz)

1 In 5-quart Dutch oven or stockpot, heat oil over medium-high heat. Add carrots, onion, celery and garlic; cook about 5 minutes, stirring frequently, until onion is tender.

2 Stir in beans, tomatoes, basil, oregano, salt, pepper and broth. Cover; simmer 30 to 45 minutes or until vegetables are tender.

3 Increase heat to medium; stir in spinach. Cover; cook 3 to 5 minutes longer or until spinach is wilted. Top individual servings with cheese.

1 Serving: Calories 270; Total Fat 6g (Saturated Fat 2g, Trans Fat 0g); Cholesterol 0mg; Sodium 990mg; Total Carbohydrate 39g (Dietary Fiber 9g); Protein 15g **Exchanges:** 2 Starch, 1 Vegetable, 1 Medium-Fat Meat **Carbohydrate Choices:** 2½

chunky tomato-bean soup

prep time: 30 Minutes || **start to finish:** 30 Minutes || 6 servings (1½ cups each)

1 tablespoon olive or vegetable oil

1 large onion, chopped (1 cup)

2 medium carrots, chopped (1 cup)

⅓ cup sun-dried tomatoes in oil, cut into thin strips

2 cans (15 oz each) cannellini beans, undrained

2 cans (14.5 oz each) diced tomatoes with basil, garlic and oregano, undrained

1 carton (32 oz) chicken broth

¼ teaspoon dried thyme leaves

⅛ teaspoon pepper

½ cup shredded Asiago cheese (2 oz)

1 In 3-quart saucepan, heat oil over medium heat. Add onion and carrots; cook about 5 minutes, stirring occasionally, until softened.

2 Stir in remaining ingredients except cheese. Heat to boiling. Reduce heat; cook uncovered 10 to 15 minutes, stirring occasionally, until vegetables are tender. Top individual servings with cheese.

1 Serving: Calories 330; Total Fat 8g (Saturated Fat 3g, Trans Fat 0g); Cholesterol 10mg; Sodium 1880mg; Total Carbohydrate 42g (Dietary Fiber 11g); Protein 21g **Exchanges:** 2½ Starch, 1 Vegetable, 1½ Medium-Fat Meat **Carbohydrate Choices:** 3

Quick Variation To make this recipe meatless, use vegetable broth in place of chicken broth.

soybean-squash soup

prep time: 20 Minutes ‖ **start to finish:** 1 Hour ‖ 4 servings (1¼ cups each)

1 tablespoon olive oil

1 large onion, chopped
(1 cup)

2 cloves garlic, finely
chopped

1 small butternut squash
(about 1¼ lb), peeled,
seeded and cubed
(about 3 cups)

1 can (15 oz) black
soybeans, drained, rinsed

1 can (14.5 oz) diced
tomatoes, undrained

1 tablespoon ground
cumin

¼ teaspoon crushed red
pepper flakes

¼ teaspoon pepper

⅛ teaspoon salt

1 cup vegetable broth
or water

1 In 5-quart Dutch oven or stockpot, heat oil over medium-high heat. Add onion and garlic; cook 3 minutes, stirring frequently, until onion is tender.

2 Stir in remaining ingredients. Heat to boiling. Reduce heat; cover and simmer 40 minutes or until squash is tender.

1 Serving: Calories 280; Total Fat 11g (Saturated Fat 1.5g, Trans Fat 0g); Cholesterol 0mg; Sodium 740mg; Total Carbohydrate 29g (Dietary Fiber 9g); Protein 15g **Exchanges:** 1 Starch, 2½ Vegetable, 1 Very Lean Meat, 2 Fat **Carbohydrate Choices:** 2

greek split pea soup

prep time: 30 Minutes ‖ **start to finish:** 1 Hour 40 Minutes ‖ 8 servings (1½ cups each)

1 bag (16 oz) dried split peas (about 2¼ cups)

2 large onions, coarsely chopped (2 cups)

3 medium stalks celery, coarsely chopped (about 1 cup)

8 cups water

2 medium red or yellow bell peppers, chopped (2 cups)

⅓ cup uncooked orzo or rosamarina pasta (about 2 oz)

¼ cup chopped fresh parsley

1 teaspoon dried oregano leaves

1 teaspoon salt

¼ teaspoon pepper

½ cup crumbled feta cheese (2 oz)

½ cup sliced ripe olives

1 In 5-quart Dutch oven or stockpot, heat split peas, onions, celery and water to boiling. Reduce heat to low; cover and simmer 1 hour to 1 hour 10 minutes or until peas are tender.

2 Puree pea mixture with immersion blender. (Or pour about 3 cups mixture into blender. Cover; blend until smooth. Pour into heatproof pitcher or bowl. Repeat with remaining mixture; return to Dutch oven.)

3 Stir in bell peppers, pasta, parsley, oregano, salt and pepper. Cook over medium heat about 15 minutes, stirring frequently so pasta does not stick to pan, or until pasta is tender. Top individual servings with cheese and olives.

1 Serving: Calories 260; Total Fat 4g (Saturated Fat 1.5g, Trans Fat 0g); Cholesterol 10mg; Sodium 500mg; Total Carbohydrate 41g (Dietary Fiber 17g); Protein 14g **Exchanges:** 2 Starch, 2 Vegetable, ½ Medium-Fat Meat **Carbohydrate Choices:** 3

bean and barley chili with cilantro sour cream

prep time: **10 Minutes** || start to finish: **1 Hour 10 Minutes** || **6 servings (1⅓ cups each)**

CHILI

- 2 tablespoons vegetable oil
- 1 large onion, chopped (1 cup)
- 2 cloves garlic, finely chopped
- ½ cup uncooked pearl barley
- 2 cups water
- 2 cans (14.5 oz each) diced tomatoes, undrained
- 2 tablespoons chili powder
- 1½ teaspoons ground cumin

  Salt and pepper, if desired
- 1 can (15 oz) black beans, drained, rinsed
- 1 can (15 oz) dark red kidney beans, drained, rinsed
- ¾ cup chunky-style salsa

CILANTRO SOUR CREAM

- ½ cup sour cream
- 2 tablespoons finely chopped fresh cilantro

1 In 5-quart Dutch oven or stockpot, heat oil over medium-high heat. Add onion and garlic; cook 5 minutes, stirring frequently, until tender. Stir in barley, water, tomatoes, chili powder, cumin, salt and pepper. Reduce heat; cover and simmer 30 minutes.

2 Stir in beans and salsa. Cook about 30 minutes longer or until barley is tender.

3 In small bowl, mix sour cream and cilantro until blended. Serve chili topped with cilantro sour cream.

1 Serving: Calories 400; Total Fat 10g (Saturated Fat 3g, Trans Fat 0g); Cholesterol 10mg; Sodium 640mg; Total Carbohydrate 61g (Dietary Fiber 17g); Protein 16g **Exchanges:** 4 Starch, 1 Vegetable, 1½ Fat **Carbohydrate Choices:** 4

thick italian winter stew
with vermicelli

prep time: **20 Minutes** ‖ start to finish: **30 Minutes** ‖ **4 servings (1½ cups each)**

½ cup 1-inch pieces uncooked vermicelli or small pasta shells (2 oz)

4 teaspoons olive oil

2 medium onions, chopped (1 cup)

½ medium green bell pepper, chopped

1 medium zucchini, cut in half lengthwise, then crosswise into thin slices (about 1½ cups)

1 can (14.5 oz) diced tomatoes with garlic, oregano and basil, undrained

1 can (14 oz) beef or vegetable broth

1 teaspoon dried Italian seasoning

1 can (15 oz) red kidney beans, drained, rinsed

2 tablespoons chopped fresh parsley

1 Cook and drain vermicelli as directed on package; cover to keep warm.

2 Meanwhile, spray 4-quart Dutch oven or saucepan with cooking spray. Add 1 teaspoon of the oil; heat over medium-high heat. Add onions and bell pepper; cook 5 minutes, stirring occasionally.

3 Stir in zucchini, tomatoes, broth and Italian seasoning. Heat to boiling over high heat. Stir in kidney beans; return just to boiling. Reduce heat to medium; cook 10 minutes.

4 Add cooked vermicelli, parsley and remaining 3 teaspoons oil to stew; stir gently to mix.

1 Serving: Calories 270; Total Fat 6g (Saturated Fat 1g, Trans Fat 0g); Cholesterol 0mg; Sodium 820mg; Total Carbohydrate 46g (Dietary Fiber 10g); Protein 14g **Exchanges:** 3 Starch, 1 Vegetable, 1 Fat **Carbohydrate Choices:** 2½

ravioli and eggplant stew

prep time: **50 Minutes** ‖ start to finish: **55 Minutes** ‖ **4 servings**

3 tablespoons olive or vegetable oil

2 cups cubed eggplant

1 can (14.5 oz) Italian-style stewed tomatoes, undrained

1½ teaspoons chopped fresh or ½ teaspoon dried basil leaves

1 cup water

1 medium zucchini, cut in half lengthwise, then crosswise into ½-inch slices (2 cups)

1 package (9 oz) refrigerated cheese-filled ravioli

1 cup shredded Parmesan cheese (4 oz)

1 In 12-inch skillet, heat oil over medium-high heat. Add eggplant; cook 5 minutes, stirring occasionally. Stir in tomatoes and basil. Heat to boiling. Reduce heat; cover and simmer about 15 minutes, stirring once or twice, until eggplant is tender.

2 Stir in water, zucchini and ravioli. Heat to boiling. Reduce heat; cover and simmer 10 minutes, stirring once or twice, until ravioli are tender.

3 Sprinkle with cheese. Cover; heat about 5 minutes or until cheese is melted.

1 Serving: Calories 370; Total Fat 22g (Saturated Fat 8g, Trans Fat 0g); Cholesterol 75mg; Sodium 1100mg; Total Carbohydrate 25g (Dietary Fiber 3g); Protein 17g **Exchanges:** 1 Starch, 2½ Vegetable, 1 Lean Meat, 3½ Fat **Carbohydrate Choices:** 1½

Quick Variation Certainly any flavor of refrigerated filled ravioli can be used. Try mushroom or chicken for a change of pace!

time-saver You can cut up the eggplant ahead of time. But be sure to either brush it with a little lemon juice or dip it into 1 quart cold water mixed with 3 tablespoons lemon juice to prevent the flesh from discoloring.

metric conversion guide

VOLUME

U.S. Units	Canadian Metric	Australian Metric
¼ teaspoon	1 mL	1 ml
½ teaspoon	2 mL	2 ml
1 teaspoon	5 mL	5 ml
1 tablespoon	15 mL	20 ml
¼ cup	50 mL	60 ml
⅓ cup	75 mL	80 ml
½ cup	125 mL	125 ml
⅔ cup	150 mL	170 ml
¾ cup	175 mL	190 ml
1 cup	250 mL	250 ml
1 quart	1 liter	1 liter
1½ quarts	1.5 liters	1.5 liters
2 quarts	2 liters	2 liters
2½ quarts	2.5 liters	2.5 liters
3 quarts	3 liters	3 liters
4 quarts	4 liters	4 liters

WEIGHT

U.S. Units	Canadian Metric	Australian Metric
1 ounce	30 grams	30 grams
2 ounces	55 grams	60 grams
3 ounces	85 grams	90 grams
4 ounces (¼ pound)	115 grams	125 grams
8 ounces (½ pound)	225 grams	225 grams
16 ounces (1 pound)	455 grams	500 grams
1 pound	455 grams	0.5 kilogram

MEASUREMENTS

Inches	Centimeters
1	2.5
2	5.0
3	7.5
4	10.0
5	12.5
6	15.0
7	17.5
8	20.5
9	23.0
10	25.5
11	28.0
12	30.5
13	33.0

TEMPERATURES

Fahrenheit	Celsius
32°	0°
212°	100°
250°	120°
275°	140°
300°	150°
325°	160°
350°	180°
375°	190°
400°	200°
425°	220°
450°	230°
475°	240°
500°	260°

Note: The recipes in this cookbook have not been developed or tested using metric measures. When converting recipes to metric, some variations in quality may be noted.

index

Page numbers in *italics* indicate illustrations

A

African Groundnut Stew with Chicken, 232

Andouille Sausage, Squash and Wild Rice Casserole, 36, *37*

Apple(s)
Cinnamon and Butternut Squash Soup, 310, *311*
Pork Chops, Smoked, with Sweet Potato and, 149
Pork, Roast, with Sweet Potatoes and, 146
'n Sausage Cheddar Biscuit Bake, 41

Artichoke(s)
-Chicken Casserole, 12, *13*
Chicken Ziti, Parmesan, with Spinach and, 182, *183*
-Spinach Lasagna, 52, *53*

Asian Beef Roast with Cabbage and Pasta, 242, *243*

Asparagus and Turkey Sausage Skillet, 188, *189*

B

Bacon
Canadian, and Lentil Soup, 253
Chicken Club Pie, Gluten-Free Impossibly Easy, 78
Chicken Thighs, Skillet, with Spinach and, 166, *167*
Kale and Tomato Mac and Cheese, 46, *47*
Pork Tenderloin, -Wrapped, with Harvest Vegetables, *145*, 145
-Potato-Onion Slab Pie, 100, *101*
-Potato Soup, Cheesy, 254, *255*
Ravioli Carbonara, Basil-Chicken, 178, *179*
-Tomato Pie, Cheesy, 99

Baked Fish Packets with Chinese Parsley Paste, 160

Balsamic Pork Chops with Quinoa, 202, *203*

Barbecue Beef and Bow-Tie Dinner, 33

Barley
and Bean Chili with Cilantro Sour Cream, 322, *323*
and Black Bean Pilaf, 226, *227*

and Chicken Risotto with Edamame, 230, *231*

Basil
-Chicken Ravioli Carbonara, 178, *179*
Pesto-Chicken Casserole, Creamy, 17
Pesto-Chicken Pot Pie, Gluten-Free Italian, 69
Salmon with Julienne Vegetables and, 221
Spaghetti Ragu with Fresh Basil, 194, *195*

Bean(s). *See also* Black Bean(s)
Burrito Pot Pies, 80, *81*
Cassoulet, Great Northern Bean and Veggie Sausage, 368, *369*
Chili, and Barley, with Cilantro Sour Cream, 322, *323*
Chili, and Beef, 288, *289*
Chili, Black Bean-Sweet Potato, 264, *265*
Chili, Chicken, White, 280, *281*
Chili, Chipotle Four-Bean, with Lime, 266
Chili, Family Favorite, *240*, 240
Chili, Nacho, Skillet, 290

Recipe Testing and Calculating Nutrition Information

Recipe Testing:

Large eggs and 2% milk were used unless otherwise indicated.

Fat-free, low-fat, low-sodium or lite products were not used unless indicated.

No nonstick cookware or bakeware was used unless otherwise indicated. No dark-colored, black or insulated bakeware was used.

When a pan is specified, a metal pan was used; a baking dish or pie plate means ovenproof glass was used.

An electric hand mixer was used for mixing only when mixer speeds are specified.

Calculating Nutrition:

The first ingredient was used wherever a choice is given, such as ⅓ cup sour cream or plain yogurt.

The first amount was used wherever a range is given, such as 3- to 3½-pound whole chicken.

The first serving number was used wherever a range is given, such as 4 to 6 servings.

"If desired" ingredients were not included.

Only the amount of a marinade or frying oil that is absorbed was included.